Lauren Wilkinson

W9-ATX-978

An Ideal Husband

Oscar Wilde

An Ideal Husband

THE PERSONS OF THE PLAY

THE EARL OF CAVERSHAM, K.G.
VISCOUNT GORING, his Son
SIR ROBERT CHILTERN, Bart., Under-Secretary for Foreign Affairs
VICOMTE DE NANJAC, Attache at the French Embassy in London
MR. MONTFORD MASON, Butler to Sir Robert Chiltern
PHIPPS, Lord Goring's Servant JAMES } HAROLD } Footmen
LADY CHILTERN
LADY MARKBY THE COUNTESS OF BASILDON
MRS. MARCHMONT
MISS MABEL CHILTERN, Sir Robert Chiltern's Sister
MRS. CHEVELEY

THE SCENES OF THE PLAY

ACT I. The Octagon Room in Sir Robert Chiltern's House in Grosvenor Square.

ACT II. Morning-room in Sir Robert Chiltern's House.

ACT III. The Library of Lord Goring's House in Curzon Street.

ACT IV. Same as Act II.

TIME: The Present

PLACE: London.

The action of the play is completed within twenty-four hours.

An Ideal Husband

FIRST ACT

SCENE

The octagon room at Sir Robert Chiltern's house in Grosvenor Square.

[The room is brilliantly lighted and full of guests. At the top of the staircase stands LADY CHILTERN, a woman of grave Greek beauty, about twenty-seven years of age. She receives the guests as they come up. Over the well of the staircase hangs a great chandelier with wax lights, which illumine a large eighteenth-century French tapestry - representing the Triumph of Love, from a design by Boucher - that is stretched on the staircase wall. On the right is the entrance to the music-room. The sound of a string quartette is faintly heard. The entrance on the left leads to other reception- rooms. MRS. MARCHMONT and LADY BASILDON, two very pretty women, are seated together on a Louis Seize sofa. They are types of exquisite fragility. Their affectation of manner has a delicate charm. Watteau would have loved to paint them.]

MRS. MARCHMONT. Going on to the Hartlocks' to-night, Margaret?

LADY BASILDON. I suppose so. Are you?

MRS. MARCHMONT. Yes. Horribly tedious parties they give, don't they?

LADY BASILDON. Horribly tedious! Never know why I go. Never know why I go anywhere.

MRS. MARCHMONT. I come here to be educated

LADY BASILDON. Ah! I hate being educated!

MRS. MARCHMONT. So do I. It puts one almost on a level with the commercial classes, doesn't it? But dear Gertrude Chiltern is always telling me that I should have some serious purpose in life. So I come here to try to find one.

LADY BASILDON. [Looking round through her lorgnette.] I don't see anybody here to-night whom one could possibly call a serious pose. The man who took me in to dinner talked to me about his wife the whole time.

MRS. MARCHMONT. How very trivial of him!

LADY BASILDON. Terribly trivial! What did your man talk about?

MRS. MARCHMONT. About myself.

LADY BASILDON. [Languidly.] And were you interested?

MRS. MARCHMONT. [Shaking her head.] Not in the smallest degree.

LADY BASILDON. What martyrs we are, dear Margaret!

MRS. MARCHMONT. [Rising.] And how well it becomes us, Olivia!

[They rise and go towards the music-room. The VICOMTE DE NANJAC, a young attache known for his neckties and his Anglomania, approaches with a low bow, and enters into conversation.]

MASON. [Announcing guests from the top of the staircase.] Mr. and Lady Jane Barford. Lord Caversham.

[Enter LORD CAVERSHAM, an old gentleman of seventy, wearing the riband and star of the Garter. A fine Whig type. Rather like a portrait by Lawrence.]

LORD CAVERSHAM. Good evening, Lady Chiltern! Has my good-for- nothing young son been here?

LADY CHILTERN. [Smiling.] I don't think Lord Goring has arrived yet.

MABEL CHILTERN. [Coming up to LORD CAVERSHAM.] Why do you call Lord Goring good-for-nothing?

[MABEL CHILTERN is a perfect example of the English type of prettiness, the apple-blossom type. She has all the fragrance and freedom of a flower. There is ripple after ripple of sunlight in her hair, and the little mouth, with its parted lips, is expectant, like the mouth of a child. She has the fascinating tyranny of youth, and the astonishing courage of innocence. To sane people she is not reminiscent of any work of art. But she is really like a Tanagra statuette, and would be rather annoyed if she were told so.]

LORD CAVERSHAM. Because he leads such an idle life.

MABEL CHILTERN. How can you say such a thing? Why, he rides in the Row at ten o'clock in the morning, goes to the Opera three times a week, changes his clothes at least five times a day, and dines out every night of the season. You don't call that leading an idle life, do you?

LORD CAVERSHAM. [Looking at her with a kindly twinkle in his eyes.] You are a very charming young lady!

MABEL CHILTERN. How sweet of you to say that, Lord Caversham! Do come to us more often. You know we are always at home on Wednesdays, and you look so well with your star!

LORD CAVERSHAM. Never go anywhere now. Sick of London Society. Shouldn't mind being introduced to my own tailor; he always votes on the right side. But object strongly to being sent down to dinner with my wife's milliner. Never could stand Lady Caversham's bonnets.

MABEL CHILTERN. Oh, I love London Society! I think it has immensely improved. It is entirely composed now of beautiful idiots and brilliant lunatics. Just what Society should be.

LORD CAVERSHAM. Hum! Which is Goring? Beautiful idiot, or the other thing?

MABEL CHILTERN. [Gravely.] I have been obliged for the present to put Lord Goring into a class quite by himself. But he is developing charmingly!

LORD CAVERSHAM. Into what?

MABEL CHILTERN. [With a little curtsey.] I hope to let you know very soon, Lord Caversham!

MASON. [Announcing guests.] Lady Markby. Mrs. Cheveley.

[Enter LADY MARKBY and MRS. CHEVELEY. LADY MARKBY is a pleasant, kindly, popular woman, with gray hair e la marquise and good lace. MRS. CHEVELEY, who accompanies her, is tall and rather slight. Lips very thin and highly-coloured, a line of scarlet on a pallid face. Venetian red hair, aquiline nose, and long throat. Rouge accentuates the natural paleness of her complexion. Gray-green eyes that move restlessly. She is in heliotrope, with diamonds. She looks rather like an orchid, and makes great demands on one's curiosity. In all her movements she is extremely graceful. A work of art, on the whole, but showing the influence of too many schools.]

LADY MARKBY. Good evening, dear Gertrude! So kind of you to let me bring my friend, Mrs. Cheveley. Two such charming women should know each other!

LADY CHILTERN. [Advances towards MRS. CHEVELEY with a sweet smile. Then suddenly stops, and bows rather distantly.] I think Mrs. Cheveley and I have met before. I did not know she had married a second time.

LADY MARKBY. [Genially.] Ah, nowadays people marry as often as they can, don't they? It is most fashionable. [To DUCHESS OF MARYBOROUGH.] Dear Duchess, and how is the Duke? Brain still weak, I suppose? Well, that is only to be expected, is it not? His good father was just the same. There is nothing like race, is there?

MRS. CHEVELEY. [Playing with her fan.] But have we really met before, Lady Chiltern? I can't remember where. I have been out of England for so long.

LADY CHILTERN. We were at school together, Mrs. Cheveley.

MRS. CHEVELEY [Superciliously.] Indeed? I have forgotten all about my schooldays. I have a vague impression that they were detestable.

LADY CHILTERN. [Coldly.] I am not surprised!

MRS. CHEVELEY. [In her sweetest manner.] Do you know, I am quite looking forward to meeting your clever husband, Lady Chiltern. Since he has been at the Foreign Office, he has been so

4

much talked of in Vienna. They actually succeed in spelling his name right in the newspapers. That in itself is fame, on the continent.

LADY CHILTERN. I hardly think there will be much in common between you and my husband, Mrs. Cheveley! [Moves away.]

VICOMTE DE NANJAC. Ah! chere Madame, queue surprise! I have not seen you since Berlin!

MRS. CHEVELEY. Not since Berlin, Vicomte. Five years ago!

VICOMTE DE NANJAC. And you are younger and more beautiful than ever. How do you manage it?

MRS. CHEVELEY. By making it a rule only to talk to perfectly charming people like yourself.

VICOMTE DE NANJAC. Ah! you flatter me. You butter me, as they say here.

MRS. CHEVELEY. Do they say that here? How dreadful of them!

VICOMTE DE NANJAC. Yes, they have a wonderful language. It should be more widely known.

[SIR ROBERT CHILTERN enters. A man of forty, but looking somewhat younger. Clean-shaven, with finely-cut features, dark-haired and dark-eyed. A personality of mark. Not popular - few personalities are. But intensely admired by the few, and deeply respected by the many. The note of his manner is that of perfect distinction, with a slight touch of pride. One feels that he is conscious of the success he has made in life. A nervous temperament, with a tired look. The firmly-chiselled mouth and chin contrast strikingly with the romantic expression in the deep-set eyes. The variance is suggestive of an almost complete separation of passion and intellect, as though thought and emotion were each isolated in its own sphere through some violence of will-power. There is nervousness in the nostrils, and in the pale, thin, pointed hands. It would be inaccurate to call him picturesque. Picturesqueness cannot survive the House of Commons. But Vandyck would have liked to have painted his head.]

SIR ROBERT CHILTERN. Good evening, Lady Markby! I hope you have brought Sir John with you?

LADY MARKBY. Oh! I have brought a much more charming person than Sir John. Sir John's temper since he has taken seriously to politics has become quite unbearable. Really, now that the House of Commons is trying to become useful, it does a great deal of harm.

SIR ROBERT CHILTERN. I hope not, Lady Markby. At any rate we do our best to waste the public time, don't we? But who is this charming person you have been kind enough to bring to us?

LADY MARKBY. Her name is Mrs. Cheveley! One of the Dorsetshire Cheveleys, I suppose. But I really don't know. Families are so mixed nowadays. Indeed, as a rule, everybody turns out to be somebody else.

SIR ROBERT CHILTERN. Mrs. Cheveley? I seem to know the name.

LADY MARKBY. She has just arrived from Vienna.

SIR ROBERT CHILTERN. Ah! yes. I think I know whom you mean.

LADY MARKBY. Oh! she goes everywhere there, and has such pleasant scandals about all her friends. I really must go to Vienna next winter. I hope there is a good chef at the Embassy.

SIR ROBERT CHILTERN. If there is not, the Ambassador will certainly have to be recalled. Pray point out Mrs. Cheveley to me. I should like to see her.

LADY MARKBY. Let me introduce you. [To MRS. CHEVELEY.] My dear, Sir Robert Chiltern is dying to know you!

SIR ROBERT CHILTERN. [Bowing.] Every one is dying to know the brilliant Mrs. Cheveley. Our attaches at Vienna write to us about nothing else.

MRS. CHEVELEY. Thank you, Sir Robert. An acquaintance that begins with a compliment is sure to develop into a real friendship. It starts in the right manner. And I find that I know Lady Chiltern already.

SIR ROBERT CHILTERN. Really?

MRS. CHEVELEY. Yes. She has just reminded me that w
school together. I remember it perfectly now. She alway
good conduct prize. I have a distinct recollection of Lady Chiltern
always getting the good conduct prize!

SIR ROBERT CHILTERN. [Smiling.] And what prizes did you get,
Mrs. Cheveley?

MRS. CHEVELEY. My prizes came a little later on in life. I don't
think any of them were for good conduct. I forget!

SIR ROBERT CHILTERN. I am sure they were for something
charming!

MRS. CHEVELEY. I don't know that women are always rewarded
for being charming. I think they are usually punished for it!
Certainly, more women grow old nowadays through the faithfulness
of their admirers than through anything else! At least that is the only
way I can account for the terribly haggard look of most of your
pretty women in London!

SIR ROBERT CHILTERN. What an appalling philosophy that
sounds! To attempt to classify you, Mrs. Cheveley, would be an
impertinence. But may I ask, at heart, are you an optimist or a
pessimist? Those seem to be the only two fashionable religions left to
us nowadays.

MRS. CHEVELEY. Oh, I'm neither. Optimism begins in a broad grin,
and Pessimism ends with blue spectacles. Besides, they are both of
them merely poses.

SIR ROBERT CHILTERN. You prefer to be natural?

MRS. CHEVELEY. Sometimes. But it is such a very difficult pose to
keep up.

SIR ROBERT CHILTERN. What would those modern psychological
novelists, of whom we hear so much, say to such a theory as that?

MRS. CHEVELEY. Ah! the strength of women comes from the fact that psychology cannot explain us. Men can be analysed, women . . . merely adored.

SIR ROBERT CHILTERN. You think science cannot grapple with the problem of women?

MRS. CHEVELEY. Science can never grapple with the irrational. That is why it has no future before it, in this world.

SIR ROBERT CHILTERN. And women represent the irrational.

MRS. CHEVELEY. Well-dressed women do.

SIR ROBERT CHILTERN. [With a polite bow.] I fear I could hardly agree with you there. But do sit down. And now tell me, what makes you leave your brilliant Vienna for our gloomy London - or perhaps the question is indiscreet?

MRS. CHEVELEY. Questions are never indiscreet. Answers sometimes are.

SIR ROBERT CHILTERN. Well, at any rate, may I know if it is politics or pleasure?

MRS. CHEVELEY. Politics are my only pleasure. You see nowadays it is not fashionable to flirt till one is forty, or to be romantic till one is forty-five, so we poor women who are under thirty, or say we are, have nothing open to us but politics or philanthropy. And philanthropy seems to me to have become simply the refuge of people who wish to annoy their fellow-creatures. I prefer politics. I think they are more . . . becoming!

SIR ROBERT CHILTERN. A political life is a noble career!

MRS. CHEVELEY. Sometimes. And sometimes it is a clever game, Sir Robert. And sometimes it is a great nuisance.

SIR ROBERT CHILTERN. Which do you find it?

MRS. CHEVELEY. I? A combination of all three. [Drops her fan.]

SIR ROBERT CHILTERN. [Picks up fan.] Allow me!

MRS. CHEVELEY. Thanks.

SIR ROBERT CHILTERN. But you have not told me yet what makes you honour London so suddenly. Our season is almost over.

MRS. CHEVELEY. Oh! I don't care about the London season! It is too matrimonial. People are either hunting for husbands, or hiding from them. I wanted to meet you. It is quite true. You know what a woman's curiosity is. Almost as great as a man's! I wanted immensely to meet you, and . . . to ask you to do something for me.

SIR ROBERT CHILTERN. I hope it is not a little thing, Mrs. Cheveley. I find that little things are so very difficult to do.

MRS. CHEVELEY. [After a moment's reflection.] No, I don't think it is quite a little thing.

SIR ROBERT CHILTERN. I am so glad. Do tell me what it is.

MRS. CHEVELEY. Later on. [Rises.] And now may I walk through your beautiful house? I hear your pictures are charming. Poor Baron Arnheim - you remember the Baron? - used to tell me you had some wonderful Corots.

SIR ROBERT CHILTERN. [With an almost imperceptible start.] Did you know Baron Arnheim well?

MRS. CHEVELEY. [Smiling.] Intimately. Did you?

SIR ROBERT CHILTERN. At one time.

MRS. CHEVELEY. Wonderful man, wasn't he?

SIR ROBERT CHILTERN. [After a pause.] He was very remarkable, in many ways.

MRS. CHEVELEY. I often think it such a pity he never wrote his memoirs. They would have been most interesting.

SIR ROBERT CHILTERN. Yes: he knew men and cities well, like the old Greek.

MRS. CHEVELEY. Without the dreadful disadvantage of having a Penelope waiting at home for him.

MASON. Lord Goring.

[Enter LORD GORING. Thirty-four, but always says he is younger. A well-bred, expressionless face. He is clever, but would not like to be thought so. A flawless dandy, he would be annoyed if he were considered romantic. He plays with life, and is on perfectly good terms with the world. He is fond of being misunderstood. It gives him a post of vantage.]

SIR ROBERT CHILTERN. Good evening, my dear Arthur! Mrs. Cheveley, allow me to introduce to you Lord Goring, the idlest man in London.

MRS. CHEVELEY. I have met Lord Goring before.

LORD GORING. [Bowing.] I did not think you would remember me, Mrs. Cheveley.

MRS. CHEVELEY. My memory is under admirable control. And are you still a bachelor?

LORD GORING. I . . . believe so.

MRS. CHEVELEY. How very romantic!

LORD GORING. Oh! I am not at all romantic. I am not old enough. I leave romance to my seniors.

SIR ROBERT CHILTERN. Lord Goring is the result of Boodle's Club, Mrs. Cheveley.

MRS. CHEVELEY. He reflects every credit on the institution.

LORD GORING. May I ask are you staying in London long?

MRS. CHEVELEY. That depends partly on the weather, partly on the cooking, and partly on Sir Robert.

SIR ROBERT CHILTERN. You are not going to plunge us into a European war, I hope?

MRS. CHEVELEY. There is no danger, at present!

[She nods to LORD GORING, with a look of amusement in her eyes, and goes out with SIR ROBERT CHILTERN. LORD GORING saunters over to MABEL CHILTERN.]

MABEL CHILTERN. You are very late!

LORD GORING. Have you missed me?

MABEL CHILTERN. Awfully!

LORD GORING. Then I am sorry I did not stay away longer. I like being missed.

MABEL CHILTERN. How very selfish of you!

LORD GORING. I am very selfish.

MABEL CHILTERN. You are always telling me of your bad qualities, Lord Goring.

LORD GORING. I have only told you half of them as yet, Miss Mabel!

MABEL CHILTERN. Are the others very bad?

LORD GORING. Quite dreadful! When I think of them at night I go to sleep at once.

MABEL CHILTERN. Well, I delight in your bad qualities. I wouldn't have you part with one of them.

LORD GORING. How very nice of you! But then you are always nice. By the way, I want to ask you a question, Miss Mabel. Who brought Mrs. Cheveley here? That woman in heliotrope, who has just gone out of the room with your brother?

MABEL CHILTERN. Oh, I think Lady Markby brought her. Why do you ask?

LORD GORING. I haven't seen her for years, that is all.

MABEL CHILTERN. What an absurd reason!

LORD GORING. All reasons are absurd.

MABEL CHILTERN. What sort of a woman is she?

LORD GORING. Oh! a genius in the daytime and a beauty at night!

MABEL CHILTERN. I dislike her already.

LORD GORING. That shows your admirable good taste.

VICOMTE DE NANJAC. [Approaching.] Ah, the English young lady is the dragon of good taste, is she not? Quite the dragon of good taste.

LORD GORING. So the newspapers are always telling us.

VICOMTE DE NANJAC. I read all your English newspapers. I find them so amusing.

LORD GORING. Then, my dear Nanjac, you must certainly read between the lines.

VICOMTE DE NANJAC. I should like to, but my professor objects. [To MABEL CHILTERN.] May I have the pleasure of escorting you to the music-room, Mademoiselle?

MABEL CHILTERN. [Looking very disappointed.] Delighted, Vicomte, quite delighted! [Turning to LORD GORING.] Aren't you coming to the music-room?

LORD GORING. Not if there is any music going on, Miss Mabel.

MABEL CHILTERN. [Severely.] The music is in German. You would not understand it.

[Goes out with the VICOMTE DE NANJAC. LORD CAVERSHAM comes up to his son.]

LORD CAVERSHAM. Well, sir! what are you doing here? Wasting your life as usual! You should be in bed, sir. You keep too late hours!

I heard of you the other night at Lady Rufford's dancing till four o'clock in the morning!

LORD GORING. Only a quarter to four, father.

LORD CAVERSHAM. Can't make out how you stand London Society. The thing has gone to the dogs, a lot of damned nobodies talking about nothing.

LORD GORING. I love talking about nothing, father. It is the only thing I know anything about.

LORD CAVERSHAM. You seem to me to be living entirely for pleasure.

LORD GORING. What else is there to live for, father? Nothing ages like happiness.

LORD CAVERSHAM. You are heartless, sir, very heartless!

LORD GORING. I hope not, father. Good evening, Lady Basildon!

LADY BASILDON. [Arching two pretty eyebrows.] Are you here? I had no idea you ever came to political parties!

LORD GORING. I adore political parties. They are the only place left to us where people don't talk politics.

LADY BASILDON. I delight in talking politics. I talk them all day long. But I can't bear listening to them. I don't know how the unfortunate men in the House stand these long debates.

LORD GORING. By never listening.

LADY BASILDON. Really?

LORD GORING. [In his most serious manner.] Of course. You see, it is a very dangerous thing to listen. If one listens one may be convinced; and a man who allows himself to be convinced by an argument is a thoroughly unreasonable person.

LADY BASILDON. Ah! that accounts for so much in men that I have never understood, and so much in women that their husbands never appreciate in them!

MRS. MARCHMONT. [With a sigh.] Our husbands never appreciate anything in us. We have to go to others for that!

LADY BASILDON. [Emphatically.] Yes, always to others, have we not?

LORD GORING. [Smiling.] And those are the views of the two ladies who are known to have the most admirable husbands in London.

MRS. MARCHMONT. That is exactly what we can't stand. My Reginald is quite hopelessly faultless. He is really unendurably so, at times! There is not the smallest element of excitement in knowing him.

LORD GORING. How terrible! Really, the thing should be more widely known!

LADY BASILDON. Basildon is quite as bad; he is as domestic as if he was a bachelor.

MRS. MARCHMONT. [Pressing LADY BASILDON'S hand.] My poor Olivia! We have married perfect husbands, and we are well punished for it.

LORD GORING. I should have thought it was the husbands who were punished.

MRS. MARCHMONT. [Drawing herself up.] Oh, dear no! They are as happy as possible! And as for trusting us, it is tragic how much they trust us.

LADY BASILDON. Perfectly tragic!

LORD GORING. Or comic, Lady Basildon?

LADY BASILDON. Certainly not comic, Lord Goring. How unkind of you to suggest such a thing!

MRS. MARCHMONT. I am afraid Lord Goring is in the camp of the enemy, as usual. I saw him talking to that Mrs. Cheveley when he came in.

LORD GORING. Handsome woman, Mrs. Cheveley!

LADY BASILDON. [Stiffly.] Please don't praise other women in our presence. You might wait for us to do that!

LORD GORING. I did wait.

MRS. MARCHMONT. Well, we are not going to praise her. I hear she went to the Opera on Monday night, and told Tommy Rufford at supper that, as far as she could see, London Society was entirely made up of dowdies and dandies.

LORD GORING. She is quite right, too. The men are all dowdies and the women are all dandies, aren't they?

MRS. MARCHMONT. [After a pause.] Oh! do you really think that is what Mrs. Cheveley meant?

LORD GORING. Of course. And a very sensible remark for Mrs. Cheveley to make, too.

[Enter MABEL CHILTERN. She joins the group.]

MABEL CHILTERN. Why are you talking about Mrs. Cheveley? Everybody is talking about Mrs. Cheveley! Lord Goring says - what did you say, Lord Goring, about Mrs. Cheveley? Oh! I remember, that she was a genius in the daytime and a beauty at night.

LADY BASILDON. What a horrid combination! So very unnatural!

MRS. MARCHMONT. [In her most dreamy manner.] I like looking at geniuses, and listening to beautiful people.

LORD GORING. Ah! that is morbid of you, Mrs. Marchmont!

MRS. MARCHMONT. [Brightening to a look of real pleasure.] I am so glad to hear you say that. Marchmont and I have been married for seven years, and he has never once told me that I was morbid. Men are so painfully unobservant!

LADY BASILDON. [Turning to her.] I have always said, dear Margaret, that you were the most morbid person in London.

MRS. MARCHMONT. Ah! but you are always sympathetic, Olivia!

MABEL CHILTERN. Is it morbid to have a desire for food? I have a great desire for food. Lord Goring, will you give me some supper?

LORD GORING. With pleasure, Miss Mabel. [Moves away with her.]

MABEL CHILTERN. How horrid you have been! You have never talked to me the whole evening!

LORD GORING. How could I? You went away with the child-diplomatist.

MABEL CHILTERN. You might have followed us. Pursuit would have been only polite. I don't think I like you at all this evening!

LORD GORING. I like you immensely.

MABEL CHILTERN. Well, I wish you'd show it in a more marked way! [They go downstairs.]

MRS. MARCHMONT. Olivia, I have a curious feeling of absolute faintness. I think I should like some supper very much. I know I should like some supper.

LADY BASILDON. I am positively dying for supper, Margaret!

MRS. MARCHMONT. Men are so horribly selfish, they never think of these things.

LADY BASILDON. Men are grossly material, grossly material!

[The VICOMTE DE NANJAC enters from the music-room with some other guests. After having carefully examined all the people present, he approaches LADY BASILDON.]

VICOMTE DE NANJAC. May I have the honour of taking you down to supper, Comtesse?

LADY BASILDON. [Coldly.] I never take supper, thank you, Vicomte. [The VICOMTE is about to retire. LADY BASILDON, seeing this, rises at once and takes his arm.] But I will come down with you with pleasure.

VICOMTE DE NANJAC. I am so fond of eating! I am very English in all my tastes.

LADY BASILDON. You look quite English, Vicomte, quite English.

[They pass out. MR. MONTFORD, a perfectly groomed young dandy, approaches MRS. MARCHMONT.]

MR. MONTFORD. Like some supper, Mrs. Marchmont?

MRS. MARCHMONT. [Languidly.] Thank you, Mr. Montford, I never touch supper. [Rises hastily and takes his arm.] But I will sit beside you, and watch you.

MR. MONTFORD. I don't know that I like being watched when I am eating!

MRS. MARCHMONT. Then I will watch some one else.

MR. MONTFORD. I don't know that I should like that either.

MRS. MARCHMONT. [Severely.] Pray, Mr. Montford, do not make these painful scenes of jealousy in public!

[They go downstairs with the other guests, passing SIR ROBERT CHILTERN and MRS. CHEVELEY, who now enter.]

SIR ROBERT CHILTERN. And are you going to any of our country houses before you leave England, Mrs. Cheveley?

MRS. CHEVELEY. Oh, no! I can't stand your English house-parties. In England people actually try to be brilliant at breakfast. That is so dreadful of them! Only dull people are brilliant at breakfast. And then the family skeleton is always reading family prayers. My stay in England really depends on you, Sir Robert. [Sits down on the sofa.]

SIR ROBERT CHILTERN. [Taking a seat beside her.] Seriously?

MRS. CHEVELEY. Quite seriously. I want to talk to you about a great political and financial scheme, about this Argentine Canal Company, in fact.

SIR ROBERT CHILTERN. What a tedious, practical subject for you to talk about, Mrs. Cheveley!

MRS. CHEVELEY. Oh, I like tedious, practical subjects. What I don't like are tedious, practical people. There is a wide difference. Besides, you are interested, I know, in International Canal schemes. You were Lord Radley's secretary, weren't you, when the Government bought the Suez Canal shares?

SIR ROBERT CHILTERN. Yes. But the Suez Canal was a very great and splendid undertaking. It gave us our direct route to India. It had imperial value. It was necessary that we should have control. This Argentine scheme is a commonplace Stock Exchange swindle.

MRS. CHEVELEY. A speculation, Sir Robert! A brilliant, daring speculation.

SIR ROBERT CHILTERN. Believe me, Mrs. Cheveley, it is a swindle. Let us call things by their proper names. It makes matters simpler. We have all the information about it at the Foreign Office. In fact, I sent out a special Commission to inquire into the matter privately, and they report that the works are hardly begun, and as for the money already subscribed, no one seems to know what has become of it. The whole thing is a second Panama, and with not a quarter of the chance of success that miserable affair ever had. I hope you have not invested in it. I am sure you are far too clever to have done that.

MRS. CHEVELEY. I have invested very largely in it.

SIR ROBERT CHILTERN. Who could have advised you to do such a foolish thing?

MRS. CHEVELEY. Your old friend - and mine.

SIR ROBERT CHILTERN. Who?

MRS. CHEVELEY. Baron Arnheim.

SIR ROBERT CHILTERN. [Frowning.] Ah! yes. I remember hearing, at the time of his death, that he had been mixed up in the whole affair.

MRS. CHEVELEY. It was his last romance. His last but one, to do him justice.

SIR ROBERT CHILTERN. [Rising.] But you have not seen my Corots yet. They are in the music-room. Corots seem to go with music, don't they? May I show them to you?

MRS. CHEVELEY. [Shaking her head.] I am not in a mood to-night for silver twilights, or rose-pink dawns. I want to talk business. [Motions to him with her fan to sit down again beside her.]

SIR ROBERT CHILTERN. I fear I have no advice to give you, Mrs. Cheveley, except to interest yourself in something less dangerous. The success of the Canal depends, of course, on the attitude of England, and I am going to lay the report of the Commissioners before the House to-morrow night.

MRS. CHEVELEY. That you must not do. In your own interests, Sir Robert, to say nothing of mine, you must not do that.

SIR ROBERT CHILTERN. [Looking at her in wonder.] In my own interests? My dear Mrs. Cheveley, what do you mean? [Sits down beside her.]

MRS. CHEVELEY. Sir Robert, I will be quite frank with you. I want you to withdraw the report that you had intended to lay before the House, on the ground that you have reasons to believe that the Commissioners have been prejudiced or misinformed, or something. Then I want you to say a few words to the effect that the Government is going to reconsider the question, and that you have reason to believe that the Canal, if completed, will be of great international value. You know the sort of things ministers say in cases of this kind. A few ordinary platitudes will do. In modern life nothing produces such an effect as a good platitude. It makes the whole world kin. Will you do that for me?

SIR ROBERT CHILTERN. Mrs. Cheveley, you cannot be serious in making me such a proposition!

MRS. CHEVELEY. I am quite serious.

SIR ROBERT CHILTERN. [Coldly.] Pray allow me to believe that you are not.

MRS. CHEVELEY. [Speaking with great deliberation and emphasis.] Ah! but I am. And if you do what I ask you, I . . . will pay you very handsomely!

SIR ROBERT CHILTERN. Pay me!

MRS. CHEVELEY. Yes.

SIR ROBERT CHILTERN. I am afraid I don't quite understand what you mean.

MRS. CHEVELEY. [Leaning back on the sofa and looking at him.] How very disappointing! And I have come all the way from Vienna in order that you should thoroughly understand me.

SIR ROBERT CHILTERN. I fear I don't.

MRS. CHEVELEY. [In her most nonchalant manner.] My dear Sir Robert, you are a man of the world, and you have your price, I suppose. Everybody has nowadays. The drawback is that most people are so dreadfully expensive. I know I am. I hope you will be more reasonable in your terms.

SIR ROBERT CHILTERN. [Rises indignantly.] If you will allow me, I will call your carriage for you. You have lived so long abroad, Mrs. Cheveley, that you seem to be unable to realise that you are talking to an English gentleman.

MRS. CHEVELEY. [Detains him by touching his arm with her fan, and keeping it there while she is talking.] I realise that I am talking to a man who laid the foundation of his fortune by selling to a Stock Exchange speculator a Cabinet secret.

SIR ROBERT CHILTERN. [Biting his lip.] What do you mean?

MRS. CHEVELEY. [Rising and facing him.] I mean that I know the real origin of your wealth and your career, and I have got your letter, too.

SIR ROBERT CHILTERN. What letter?

MRS. CHEVELEY. [Contemptuously.] The letter you wrote to Baron Arnheim, when you were Lord Radley's secretary, telling the Baron to buy Suez Canal shares - a letter written three days before the Government announced its own purchase.

SIR ROBERT CHILTERN. [Hoarsely.] It is not true.

MRS. CHEVELEY. You thought that letter had been destroyed. How foolish of you! It is in my possession.

SIR ROBERT CHILTERN. The affair to which you allude was no more than a speculation. The House of Commons had not yet passed the bill; it might have been rejected.

MRS. CHEVELEY. It was a swindle, Sir Robert. Let us call things by their proper names. It makes everything simpler. And now I am going to sell you that letter, and the price I ask for it is your public support of the Argentine scheme. You made your own fortune out of one canal. You must help me and my friends to make our fortunes out of another!

SIR ROBERT CHILTERN. It is infamous, what you propose - infamous!

MRS. CHEVELEY. Oh, no! This is the game of life as we all have to play it, Sir Robert, sooner or later!

SIR ROBERT CHILTERN. I cannot do what you ask me.

MRS. CHEVELEY. You mean you cannot help doing it. You know you are standing on the edge of a precipice. And it is not for you to make terms. It is for you to accept them. Supposing you refuse -

SIR ROBERT CHILTERN. What then?

MRS. CHEVELEY. My dear Sir Robert, what then? You are ruined, that is all! Remember to what a point your Puritanism in England has brought you. In old days nobody pretended to be a bit better than his neighbours. In fact, to be a bit better than one's neighbour was considered excessively vulgar and middle-class. Nowadays, with our modern mania for morality, every one has to pose as a paragon of purity, incorruptibility, and all the other seven deadly virtues - and what is the result? You all go over like ninepins - one after the other. Not a year passes in England without somebody disappearing. Scandals used to lend charm, or at least interest, to a man - now they crush him. And yours is a very nasty scandal. You couldn't survive it. If it were known that as a young man, secretary to a great and important minister, you sold a Cabinet secret for a large sum of money, and that that was the origin of your wealth and career, you would be hounded out of public life, you would disappear completely. And after all, Sir Robert, why should you sacrifice your entire future rather than deal diplomatically with your enemy? For the moment I am your enemy. I admit it! And I am much stronger than you are. The big battalions are on my side. You have a splendid position, but it is your splendid position that makes you so vulnerable. You can't defend it! And I am in attack. Of course I have not talked morality to you. You must admit in fairness that I have spared you that. Years ago you did a clever, unscrupulous thing; it turned out a great success. You owe to it your fortune and position. And now you have got to pay for it. Sooner or later we have all to pay for what we do. You have to pay now. Before I leave you to-night, you have got to promise me to suppress your report, and to speak in the House in favour of this scheme.

SIR ROBERT CHILTERN. What you ask is impossible.

MRS. CHEVELEY. You must make it possible. You are going to make it possible. Sir Robert, you know what your English newspapers are like. Suppose that when I leave this house I drive down to some newspaper office, and give them this scandal and the proofs of it! Think of their loathsome joy, of the delight they would have in dragging you down, of the mud and mire they would plunge you in. Think of the hypocrite with his greasy smile penning his leading article, and arranging the foulness of the public placard.

SIR ROBERT CHILTERN. Stop! You want me to withdraw the report and to make a short speech stating that I believe there are possibilities in the scheme?

MRS. CHEVELEY. [Sitting down on the sofa.] Those are my terms.

SIR ROBERT CHILTERN. [In a low voice.] I will give you any sum of money you want.

MRS. CHEVELEY. Even you are not rich enough, Sir Robert, to buy back your past. No man is.

SIR ROBERT CHILTERN. I will not do what you ask me. I will not.

MRS. CHEVELEY. You have to. If you don't . . . [Rises from the sofa.]

SIR ROBERT CHILTERN. [Bewildered and unnerved.] Wait a moment! What did you propose? You said that you would give me back my letter, didn't you?

MRS. CHEVELEY. Yes. That is agreed. I will be in the Ladies' Gallery to-morrow night at half-past eleven. If by that time - and you will have had heaps of opportunity - you have made an announcement to the House in the terms I wish, I shall hand you back your letter with the prettiest thanks, and the best, or at any rate the most suitable, compliment I can think of. I intend to play quite fairly with you. One should always play fairly . . . when one has the winning cards. The Baron taught me that . . . amongst other things.

SIR ROBERT CHILTERN. You must let me have time to consider your proposal.

MRS. CHEVELEY. No; you must settle now!

SIR ROBERT CHILTERN. Give me a week - three days!

MRS. CHEVELEY. Impossible! I have got to telegraph to Vienna to-night.

SIR ROBERT CHILTERN. My God! what brought you into my life?

MRS. CHEVELEY. Circumstances. [Moves towards the door.]

SIR ROBERT CHILTERN. Don't go. I consent. The report shall be withdrawn. I will arrange for a question to be put to me on the subject.

MRS. CHEVELEY. Thank you. I knew we should come to an amicable agreement. I understood your nature from the first. I analysed you, though you did not adore me. And now you can get my carriage for me, Sir Robert. I see the people coming up from supper, and Englishmen always get romantic after a meal, and that bores me dreadfully. [Exit SIR ROBERT CHILTERN.]

[Enter Guests, LADY CHILTERN, LADY MARKBY, LORD CAVERSHAM, LADY BASILDON, MRS. MARCHMONT, VICOMTE DE NANJAC, MR. MONTFORD.]

LADY MARKBY. Well, dear Mrs. Cheveley, I hope you have enjoyed yourself. Sir Robert is very entertaining, is he not?

MRS. CHEVELEY. Most entertaining! I have enjoyed my talk with him immensely.

LADY MARKBY. He has had a very interesting and brilliant career. And he has married a most admirable wife. Lady Chiltern is a woman of the very highest principles, I am glad to say. I am a little too old now, myself, to trouble about setting a good example, but I always admire people who do. And Lady Chiltern has a very ennobling effect on life, though her dinner-parties are rather dull sometimes. But one can't have everything, can one? And now I must go, dear. Shall I call for you to-morrow?

MRS. CHEVELEY. Thanks.

LADY MARKBY. We might drive in the Park at five. Everything looks so fresh in the Park now!

MRS. CHEVELEY. Except the people!

LADY MARKBY. Perhaps the people are a little jaded. I have often observed that the Season as it goes on produces a kind of softening of the brain. However, I think anything is better than high intellectual pressure. That is the most unbecoming thing there is. It makes the noses of the young girls so particularly large. And there is nothing so difficult to marry as a large nose; men don't like them. Good-night, dear! [To LADY CHILTERN.] Good-night, Gertrude! [Goes out on LORD CAVERSHAM'S arm.]

MRS. CHEVELEY. What a charming house you have, Lady Chiltern! I have spent a delightful evening. It has been so interesting getting to know your husband.

LADY CHILTERN. Why did you wish to meet my husband, Mrs. Cheveley?

MRS. CHEVELEY. Oh, I will tell you. I wanted to interest him in this Argentine Canal scheme, of which I dare say you have heard. And I found him most susceptible, - susceptible to reason, I mean. A rare thing in a man. I converted him in ten minutes. He is going to make a speech in the House to-morrow night in favour of the idea. We must go to the Ladies' Gallery and hear him! It will be a great occasion!

LADY CHILTERN. There must be some mistake. That scheme could never have my husband's support.

MRS. CHEVELEY. Oh, I assure you it's all settled. I don't regret my tedious journey from Vienna now. It has been a great success. But, of course, for the next twenty-four hours the whole thing is a dead secret.

LADY CHILTERN. [Gently.] A secret? Between whom?

MRS. CHEVELEY. [With a flash of amusement in her eyes.] Between your husband and myself.

SIR ROBERT CHILTERN. [Entering.] Your carriage is here, Mm Cheveley!

MRS. CHEVELEY. Thanks! Good evening, Lady Chiltern! Good-night, Lord Goring! I am at Claridge's. Don't you think you might leave a card?

LORD GORING. If you wish it, Mrs. Cheveley!

MRS. CHEVELEY. Oh, don't be so solemn about it, or I shall be obliged to leave a card on you. In England I suppose that would hardly be considered EN REGLE. Abroad, we are more civilised. Will you see me down, Sir Robert? Now that we have both the same interests at heart we shall be great friends, I hope!

[Sails out on SIR ROBERT CHILTERN'S arm. LADY CHILTERN goes to the top of the staircase and looks down at them as they descend. Her expression is troubled. After a little time she is joined by some of the guests, and passes with them into another reception-room.]

MABEL CHILTERN. What a horrid woman!

LORD GORING. You should go to bed, Miss Mabel.

MABEL CHILTERN. Lord Goring!

LORD GORING. My father told me to go to bed an hour ago. I don't see why I shouldn't give you the same advice. I always pass on good advice. It is the only thing to do with it. It is never of any use to oneself.

MABEL CHILTERN. Lord Goring, you are always ordering me out of the room. I think it most courageous of you. Especially as I am not going to bed for hours. [Goes over to the sofa.] You can come and sit down if you like, and talk about anything in the world, except the Royal Academy, Mrs. Cheveley, or novels in Scotch dialect. They are not improving subjects. [Catches sight of something that is lying on the sofa half hidden by the cushion.] What is this? Some one has dropped a diamond brooch! Quite beautiful, isn't it? [Shows it to him.] I wish it was mine, but Gertrude won't let me wear anything but pearls, and I am thoroughly sick of pearls. They make one look so plain, so good and so intellectual. I wonder whom the brooch belongs to.

LORD GORING. I wonder who dropped it.

MABEL CHILTERN. It is a beautiful brooch.

LORD GORING. It is a handsome bracelet.

MABEL CHILTERN. It isn't a bracelet. It's a brooch.

LORD GORING. It can be used as a bracelet. [Takes it from her, and, pulling out a green letter-case, puts the ornament carefully in it, and replaces the whole thing in his breast-pocket with the most perfect sang froid.]

MABEL CHILTERN. What are you doing?

LORD GORING. Miss Mabel, I am going to make a rather strange request to you.

MABEL CHILTERN. [Eagerly.] Oh, pray do! I have been waiting for it all the evening.

LORD GORING. [Is a little taken aback, but recovers himself.] Don't mention to anybody that I have taken charge of this brooch. Should any one write and claim it, let me know at once.

MABEL CHILTERN. That is a strange request.

LORD GORING. Well, you see I gave this brooch to somebody once, years ago.

MABEL CHILTERN. You did?

LORD GORING. Yes.

[LADY CHILTERN enters alone. The other guests have gone.]

MABEL CHILTERN. Then I shall certainly bid you good-night. Good- night, Gertrude! [Exit.]

LADY CHILTERN. Good-night, dear! [To LORD GORING.] You saw whom Lady Markby brought here to-night?

LORD GORING. Yes. It was an unpleasant surprise. What did she come here for?

LADY CHILTERN. Apparently to try and lure Robert to uphold some fraudulent scheme in which she is interested. The Argentine Canal, in fact.

LORD GORING. She has mistaken her man, hasn't she?

LADY CHILTERN. She is incapable of understanding an upright nature like my husband's!

LORD GORING. Yes. I should fancy she came to grief if she tried to get Robert into her toils. It is extraordinary what astounding mistakes clever women make.

LADY CHILTERN. I don't call women of that kind clever. I call them stupid!

LORD GORING. Same thing often. Good-night, Lady Chiltern!

LADY CHILTERN. Good-night!

[Enter SIR ROBERT CHILTERN.]

SIR ROBERT CHILTERN. My dear Arthur, you are not going? Do stop a little!

LORD GORING. Afraid I can't, thanks. I have promised to look in at the Hartlocks'. I believe they have got a mauve Hungarian band that plays mauve Hungarian music. See you soon. Good-bye!

[Exit]

SIR ROBERT CHILTERN. How beautiful you look to-night, Gertrude!

LADY CHILTERN. Robert, it is not true, is it? You are not going to lend your support to this Argentine speculation? You couldn't!

SIR ROBERT CHILTERN. [Starting.] Who told you I intended to do so?

LADY CHILTERN. That woman who has just gone out, Mrs. Cheveley, as she calls herself now. She seemed to taunt me with it. Robert, I know this woman. You don't. We were at school together. She was untruthful, dishonest, an evil influence on every one whose trust or friendship she could win. I hated, I despised her. She stole things, she was a thief. She was sent away for being a thief. Why do you let her influence you?

SIR ROBERT CHILTERN. Gertrude, what you tell me may be true, but it happened many years ago. It is best forgotten! Mrs. Cheveley may have changed since then. No one should be entirely judged by their past.

LADY CHILTERN. [Sadly.] One's past is what one is. It is the only way by which people should be judged.

SIR ROBERT CHILTERN. That is a hard saying, Gertrude!

LADY CHILTERN. It is a true saying, Robert. And what did she mean by boasting that she had got you to lend your support, your name, to a thing I have heard you describe as the most dishonest and fraudulent scheme there has ever been in political life?

SIR ROBERT CHILTERN. [Biting his lip.] I was mistaken in the view I took. We all may make mistakes.

LADY CHILTERN. But you told me yesterday that you had received the report from the Commission, and that it entirely condemned the whole thing.

SIR ROBERT CHILTERN. [Walking up and down.] I have reasons now to believe that the Commission was prejudiced, or, at any rate, misinformed. Besides, Gertrude, public and private life are different things. They have different laws, and move on different lines.

LADY CHILTERN. They should both represent man at his highest. I see no difference between them.

SIR ROBERT CHILTERN. [Stopping.] In the present case, on a matter of practical politics, I have changed my mind. That is all.

LADY CHILTERN. All!

SIR ROBERT CHILTERN. [Sternly.] Yes!

LADY CHILTERN. Robert! Oh! it is horrible that I should have to ask you such a question - Robert, are you telling me the whole truth?

SIR ROBERT CHILTERN. Why do you ask me such a question?

LADY CHILTERN. [After a pause.] Why do you not answer it?

SIR ROBERT CHILTERN. [Sitting down.] Gertrude, truth is a very complex thing, and politics is a very complex business. There are wheels within wheels. One may be under certain obligations to people that one must pay. Sooner or later in political life one has to compromise. Every one does.

LADY CHILTERN. Compromise? Robert, why do you talk so differently to-night from the way I have always heard you talk? Why are you changed?

SIR ROBERT CHILTERN. I am not changed. But circumstances alter things.

LADY CHILTERN. Circumstances should never alter principles!

SIR ROBERT CHILTERN. But if I told you -

LADY CHILTERN. What?

SIR ROBERT CHILTERN. That it was necessary, vitally necessary?

LADY CHILTERN. It can never be necessary to do what is not honourable. Or if it be necessary, then what is it that I have loved! But it is not, Robert; tell me it is not. Why should it be? What gain would you get ? Money? We have no need of that! And money that comes from a tainted source is a degradation. Power? But power is nothing in itself. It is power to do good that is fine - that, and that only. What is it, then? Robert, tell me why you are going to do this dishonourable thing!

SIR ROBERT CHILTERN. Gertrude, you have no right to use that word. I told you it was a question of rational compromise. It is no more than that.

LADY CHILTERN. Robert, that is all very well for other men, for men who treat life simply as a sordid speculation; but not for you, Robert, not for you. You are different. All your life you have stood apart from others. You have never let the world soil you. To the world, as to myself, you have been an ideal always. Oh! be that ideal still. That great inheritance throw not away - that tower of ivory do not destroy. Robert, men can love what is beneath them - things unworthy, stained, dishonoured. We women worship when we love; and when we lose our worship, we lose everything. Oh! don't kill my love for you, don't kill that!

SIR ROBERT CHILTERN. Gertrude!

LADY CHILTERN. I know that there are men with horrible secrets in their lives - men who have done some shameful thing, and who in some critical moment have to pay for it, by doing some other act of shame - oh! don't tell me you are such as they are! Robert, is there in your life any secret dishonour or disgrace? Tell me, tell me at once, that -

SIR ROBERT CHILTERN. That what?

LADY CHILTERN. [Speaking very slowly.] That our lives may drift apart.

SIR ROBERT CHILTERN. Drift apart?

LADY CHILTERN. That they may be entirely separate. It would be better for us both.

SIR ROBERT CHILTERN. Gertrude, there is nothing in my past life that you might not know.

LADY CHILTERN. I was sure of it, Robert, I was sure of it. But why did you say those dreadful things, things so unlike your real self? Don't let us ever talk about the subject again. You will write, won't you, to Mrs. Cheveley, and tell her that you cannot support this scandalous scheme of hers? If you have given her any promise you must take it back, that is all!

SIR ROBERT CHILTERN. Must I write and tell her that?

LADY CHILTERN. Surely, Robert! What else is there to do?

SIR ROBERT CHILTERN. I might see her personally. It would be better.

LADY CHILTERN. You must never see her again, Robert. She is not a woman you should ever speak to. She is not worthy to talk to a man like you. No; you must write to her at once, now, this moment, and let your letter show her that your decision is quite irrevocable!

SIR ROBERT CHILTERN. Write this moment!

LADY CHILTERN. Yes.

SIR ROBERT CHILTERN. But it is so late. It is close on twelve.

LADY CHILTERN. That makes no matter. She must know at once that she has been mistaken in you - and that you are not a man to do anything base or underhand or dishonourable. Write here, Robert. Write that you decline to support this scheme of hers, as you hold it to be a dishonest scheme. Yes - write the word dishonest. She knows what that word means. [SIR ROBERT CHILTERN sits down and writes a letter. His wife takes it up and reads it.] Yes; that will do. [Rings bell.] And now the envelope. [He writes the envelope slowly. Enter MASON.] Have this letter sent at once to Claridge's Hotel. There is no answer. [Exit MASON. LADY CHILTERN kneels down beside her husband, and puts her arms around him.] Robert, love gives one an instinct to things. I feel to-night that I have saved you from something that might have been a danger to you, from something that might have made men honour you less than they do. I don't think you realise sufficiently, Robert, that you have brought into the political life of our time a nobler atmosphere, a finer attitude towards life, a freer air of purer aims and higher ideals - I know it, and for that I love you, Robert.

SIR ROBERT CHILTERN. Oh, love me always, Gertrude, love me always!

LADY CHILTERN. I will love you always, because you will always be worthy of love. We needs must love the highest when we see it! [Kisses him and rises and goes out.]

[SIR ROBERT CHILTERN walks up and down for a moment; then sits down and buries his face in his hands. The Servant enters and begins pulling out the lights. SIR ROBERT CHILTERN looks up.]

SIR ROBERT CHILTERN. Put out the lights, Mason, put out the lights!

[The Servant puts out the lights. The room becomes almost dark. The only light there is comes from the great chandelier that hangs over the staircase and illumines the tapestry of the Triumph of Love.]

ACT DROP

An Ideal Husband

SECOND ACT

SCENE

Morning-room at Sir Robert Chiltern's house.

[LORD GORING, dressed in the height of fashion, is lounging in an armchair. SIR ROBERT CHILTERN is standing in front of the fireplace. He is evidently in a state of great mental excitement and distress. As the scene progresses he paces nervously up and down the room.]

LORD GORING. My dear Robert, it's a very awkward business, very awkward indeed. You should have told your wife the whole thing. Secrets from other people's wives are a necessary luxury in modern life. So, at least, I am always told at the club by people who are bald enough to know better. But no man should have a secret from his own wife. She invariably finds it out. Women have a wonderful instinct about things. They can discover everything except the obvious.

SIR ROBERT CHILTERN. Arthur, I couldn't tell my wife. When could I have told her? Not last night. It would have made a life-long separation between us, and I would have lost the love of the one woman in the world I worship, of the only woman who has ever stirred love within me. Last night it would have been quite impossible. She would have turned from me in horror . . . in horror and in contempt.

LORD GORING. Is Lady Chiltern as perfect as all that?

SIR ROBERT CHILTERN. Yes; my wife is as perfect as all that.

LORD GORING. [Taking off his left-hand glove.] What a pity! I beg your pardon, my dear fellow, I didn't quite mean that. But if what you tell me is true, I should like to have a serious talk about life with Lady Chiltern.

SIR ROBERT CHILTERN. It would be quite useless.

LORD GORING. May I try?

SIR ROBERT CHILTERN. Yes; but nothing could make her alter her views.

LORD GORING. Well, at the worst it would simply be a psychological experiment.

SIR ROBERT CHILTERN. All such experiments are terribly dangerous.

LORD GORING. Everything is dangerous, my dear fellow. If it wasn't so, life wouldn't be worth living. . . . Well, I am bound to say that I think you should have told her years ago.

SIR ROBERT CHILTERN. When? When we were engaged? Do you think she would have married me if she had known that the origin of my fortune is such as it is, the basis of my career such as it is, and that I had done a thing that I suppose most men would call shameful and dishonourable?

LORD GORING. [Slowly.] Yes; most men would call it ugly names. There is no doubt of that.

SIR ROBERT CHILTERN. [Bitterly.] Men who every day do something of the same kind themselves. Men who, each one of them, have worse secrets in their own lives.

LORD GORING. That is the reason they are so pleased to find out other people's secrets. It distracts public attention from their own.

SIR ROBERT CHILTERN. And, after all, whom did I wrong by what I did? No one.

LORD GORING. [Looking at him steadily.] Except yourself, Robert.

SIR ROBERT CHILTERN. [After a pause.] Of course I had private information about a certain transaction contemplated by the Government of the day, and I acted on it. Private information is practically the source of every large modern fortune.

LORD GORING. [Tapping his boot with his cane.] And public scandal invariably the result.

SIR ROBERT CHILTERN. [Pacing up and down the room.] Arthur, do you think that what I did nearly eighteen years ago should be brought up against me now? Do you think it fair that a man's whole career should be ruined for a fault done in one's boyhood almost? I was twenty-two at the time, and I had the double misfortune of being well-born and poor, two unforgiveable things nowadays. Is it fair that the folly, the sin of one's youth, if men choose to call it a sin, should wreck a life like mine, should place me in the pillory, should shatter all that I have worked for, all that I have built up. Is it fair, Arthur?

LORD GORING. Life is never fair, Robert. And perhaps it is a good thing for most of us that it is not.

SIR ROBERT CHILTERN. Every man of ambition has to fight his century with its own weapons. What this century worships is wealth. The God of this century is wealth. To succeed one must have wealth. At all costs one must have wealth.

LORD GORING. You underrate yourself, Robert. Believe me, without wealth you could have succeeded just as well.

SIR ROBERT CHILTERN. When I was old, perhaps. When I had lost my passion for power, or could not use it. When I was tired, worn out, disappointed. I wanted my success when I was young. Youth is the time for success. I couldn't wait.

LORD GORING. Well, you certainly have had your success while you are still young. No one in our day has had such a brilliant success. Under-Secretary for Foreign Affairs at the age of forty - that's good enough for any one, I should think.

SIR ROBERT CHILTERN. And if it is all taken away from me now? If I lose everything over a horrible scandal? If I am hounded from public life?

LORD GORING. Robert, how could you have sold yourself for money?

SIR ROBERT CHILTERN. [Excitedly.] I did not sell myself for money. I bought success at a great price. That is all.

LORD GORING. [Gravely.] Yes; you certainly paid a great price for it. But what first made you think of doing such a thing?

SIR ROBERT CHILTERN. Baron Arnheim.

LORD GORING. Damned scoundrel!

SIR ROBERT CHILTERN. No; he was a man of a most subtle and refined intellect. A man of culture, charm, and distinction. One of the most intellectual men I ever met.

LORD GORING. Ah! I prefer a gentlemanly fool any day. There is more to be said for stupidity than people imagine. Personally I have a great admiration for stupidity. It is a sort of fellow-feeling, I suppose. But how did he do it? Tell me the whole thing.

SIR ROBERT CHILTERN. [Throws himself into an armchair by the writing-table.] One night after dinner at Lord Radley's the Baron began talking about success in modern life as something that one could reduce to an absolutely definite science. With that wonderfully fascinating quiet voice of his he expounded to us the most terrible of all philosophies, the philosophy of power, preached to us the most marvellous of all gospels, the gospel of gold. I think he saw the effect he had produced on me, for some days afterwards he wrote and asked me to come and see him. He was living then in Park Lane, in the house Lord Woolcomb has now. I remember so well how, with a strange smile on his pale, curved lips, he led me through his wonderful picture gallery, showed me his tapestries, his enamels, his jewels, his carved ivories, made me wonder at the strange loveliness of the luxury in which he lived; and then told me that luxury was nothing but a background, a painted scene in a play, and that power, power over other men, power over the world, was the one thing worth having, the one supreme pleasure worth knowing, the one joy one never tired of, and that in our century only the rich possessed it.

LORD GORING. [With great deliberation.] A thoroughly shallow creed.

SIR ROBERT CHILTERN. [Rising.] I didn't think so then. I don't think so now. Wealth has given me enormous power. It gave me at the very outset of my life freedom, and freedom is everything. You have never been poor, and never known what ambition is. You cannot understand what a wonderful chance the Baron gave me. Such a chance as few men get.

LORD GORING. Fortunately for them, if one is to judge by results. But tell me definitely, how did the Baron finally persuade you to - well, to do what you did?

SIR ROBERT CHILTERN. When I was going away he said to me that if I ever could give him any private information of real value he would make me a very rich man. I was dazed at the prospect he held out to me, and my ambition and my desire for power were at that time boundless. Six weeks later certain private documents passed through my hands.

LORD GORING. [Keeping his eyes steadily fixed on the carpet.] State documents?

SIR ROBERT CHILTERN. Yes. [LORD GORING sighs, then passes his hand across his forehead and looks up.]

LORD GORING. I had no idea that you, of all men in the world, could have been so weak, Robert, as to yield to such a temptation as Baron Arnheim held out to you.

SIR ROBERT CHILTERN. Weak? Oh, I am sick of hearing that phrase. Sick of using it about others. Weak? Do you really think, Arthur, that it is weakness that yields to temptation? I tell you that there are terrible temptations that it requires strength, strength and courage, to yield to. To stake all one's life on a single moment, to risk everything on one throw, whether the stake be power or pleasure, I care not - there is no weakness in that. There is a horrible, a terrible courage. I had that courage. I sat down the same afternoon and wrote Baron Arnheim the letter this woman now holds. He made three-quarters of a million over the transaction

LORD GORING. And you?

SIR ROBERT CHILTERN. I received from the Baron 110,000 pounds.

LORD GORING. You were worth more, Robert.

SIR ROBERT CHILTERN. No; that money gave me exactly what I wanted, power over others. I went into the House immediately. The

Baron advised me in finance from time to time. Before five years I had almost trebled my fortune. Since then everything that I have touched has turned out a success. In all things connected with money I have had a luck so extraordinary that sometimes it has made me almost afraid. I remember having read somewhere, in some strange book, that when the gods wish to punish us they answer our prayers.

LORD GORING. But tell me, Robert, did you never suffer any regret for what you had done?

SIR ROBERT CHILTERN. No. I felt that I had fought the century with its own weapons, and won.

LORD GORING. [Sadly.] You thought you had won.

SIR ROBERT CHILTERN. I thought so. [After a long pause.] Arthur, do you despise me for what I have told you?

LORD GORING. [With deep feeling in his voice.] I am very sorry for you, Robert, very sorry indeed.

SIR ROBERT CHILTERN. I don't say that I suffered any remorse. I didn't. Not remorse in the ordinary, rather silly sense of the word. But I have paid conscience money many times. I had a wild hope that I might disarm destiny. The sum Baron Arnheim gave me I have distributed twice over in public charities since then.

LORD GORING. [Looking up.] In public charities? Dear me! what a lot of harm you must have done, Robert!

SIR ROBERT CHILTERN. Oh, don't say that, Arthur; don't talk like that!

LORD GORING. Never mind what I say, Robert! I am always saying what I shouldn't say. In fact, I usually say what I really think. A great mistake nowadays. It makes one so liable to be misunderstood. As regards this dreadful business, I will help you in whatever way I can. Of course you know that.

SIR ROBERT CHILTERN. Thank you, Arthur, thank you. But what is to be done? What can be done?

LORD GORING. [Leaning back with his hands in his pockets.] Well, the English can't stand a man who is always saying he is in the right, but they are very fond of a man who admits that he has been in the wrong. It is one of the best things in them. However, in your case, Robert, a confession would not do. The money, if you will allow me to say so, is . . . awkward. Besides, if you did make a clean breast of the whole affair, you would never be able to talk morality again. And in England a man who can't talk morality twice a week to a large, popular, immoral audience is quite over as a serious politician. There would be nothing left for him as a profession except Botany or the Church. A confession would be of no use. It would ruin you.

SIR ROBERT CHILTERN. It would ruin me. Arthur, the only thing for me to do now is to fight the thing out.

LORD GORING. [Rising from his chair.] I was waiting for you to say that, Robert. It is the only thing to do now. And you must begin by telling your wife the whole story.

SIR ROBERT CHILTERN. That I will not do.

LORD GORING. Robert, believe me, you are wrong.

SIR ROBERT CHILTERN. I couldn't do it. It would kill her love for me. And now about this woman, this Mrs. Cheveley. How can I defend myself against her? You knew her before, Arthur, apparently.

LORD GORING. Yes.

SIR ROBERT CHILTERN. Did you know her well?

LORD GORING. [Arranging his necktie.] So little that I got engaged to be married to her once, when I was staying at the Tenbys'. The affair lasted for three days . . . nearly.

SIR ROBERT CHILTERN. Why was it broken off?

LORD GORING. [Airily.] Oh, I forget. At least, it makes no matter. By the way, have you tried her with money? She used to be confoundedly fond of money.

SIR ROBERT CHILTERN. I offered her any sum she wanted. She refused.

LORD GORING. Then the marvellous gospel of gold breaks down sometimes. The rich can't do everything, after all.

SIR ROBERT CHILTERN. Not everything. I suppose you are right. Arthur, I feel that public disgrace is in store for me. I feel certain of it. I never knew what terror was before. I know it now. It is as if a hand of ice were laid upon one's heart. It is as if one's heart were beating itself to death in some empty hollow.

LORD GORING. [Striking the table.] Robert, you must fight her. You must fight her.

SIR ROBERT CHILTERN. But how?

LORD GORING. I can't tell you how at present. I have not the smallest idea. But every one has some weak point. There is some flaw in each one of us. [Strolls to the fireplace and looks at himself in the glass.] My father tells me that even I have faults. Perhaps I have. I don't know.

SIR ROBERT CHILTERN. In defending myself against Mrs. Cheveley, I have a right to use any weapon I can find, have I not?

LORD GORING. [Still looking in the glass.] In your place I don't think I should have the smallest scruple in doing so. She is thoroughly well able to take care of herself.

SIR ROBERT CHILTERN. [Sits down at the table and takes a pen in his hand.] Well, I shall send a cipher telegram to the Embassy at Vienna, to inquire if there is anything known against her. There may be some secret scandal she might be afraid of.

LORD GORING. [Settling his buttonhole.] Oh, I should fancy Mrs. Cheveley is one of those very modern women of our time who find a new scandal as becoming as a new bonnet, and air them both in the Park every afternoon at five-thirty. I am sure she adores scandals, and that the sorrow of her life at present is that she can't manage to have enough of them.

SIR ROBERT CHILTERN. [Writing.] Why do you say that?

LORD GORING. [Turning round.] Well, she wore far too much rouge last night, and not quite enough clothes. That is always a sign of despair in a woman.

SIR ROBERT CHILTERN. [Striking a bell.] But it is worth while my wiring to Vienna, is it not?

LORD GORING. It is always worth while asking a question, though it is not always worth while answering one.

[Enter MASON.]

SIR ROBERT CHILTERN. Is Mr. Trafford in his room?

MASON. Yes, Sir Robert.

SIR ROBERT CHILTERN. [Puts what he has written into an envelope, which he then carefully closes.] Tell him to have this sent off in cipher at once. There must not be a moment's delay.

MASON. Yes, Sir Robert.

SIR ROBERT CHILTERN. Oh! just give that back to me again.

[Writes something on the envelope. MASON then goes out with the letter.]

SIR ROBERT CHILTERN. She must have had some curious hold over Baron Arnheim. I wonder what it was.

LORD GORING. [Smiling.] I wonder.

SIR ROBERT CHILTERN. I will fight her to the death, as long as my wife knows nothing.

LORD GORING. [Strongly.] Oh, fight in any case - in any case.

SIR ROBERT CHILTERN. [With a gesture of despair.] If my wife found out, there would be little left to fight for. Well, as soon as I hear from Vienna, I shall let you know the result. It is a chance, just a chance, but I believe in it. And as I fought the age with its own weapons, I will fight her with her weapons. It is only fair, and she looks like a woman with a past, doesn't she?

LORD GORING. Most pretty women do. But there is a fashion in pasts just as there is a fashion in frocks. Perhaps Mrs. Cheveley's past is merely a slightly DECOLLETE one, and they are excessively popular nowadays. Besides, my dear Robert, I should not build too high hopes on frightening Mrs. Cheveley. I should not fancy Mrs. Cheveley is a woman who would be easily frightened. She has survived all her creditors, and she shows wonderful presence of mind.

SIR ROBERT CHILTERN. Oh! I live on hopes now. I clutch at every chance. I feel like a man on a ship that is sinking. The water is round my feet, and the very air is bitter with storm. Hush! I hear my wife's voice.

[Enter LADY CHILTERN in walking dress.]

LADY CHILTERN. Good afternoon, Lord Goring!

LORD GORING. Good afternoon, Lady Chiltern! Have you been in the Park?

LADY CHILTERN. No; I have just come from the Woman's Liberal Association, where, by the way, Robert, your name was received with loud applause, and now I have come in to have my tea. [To LORD GORING.] You will wait and have some tea, won't you?

LORD GORING. I'll wait for a short time, thanks.

LADY CHILTERN. I will be back in a moment. I am only going to take my hat off.

LORD GORING. [In his most earnest manner.] Oh! please don't. It is so pretty. One of the prettiest hats I ever saw. I hope the Woman's Liberal Association received it with loud applause.

LADY CHILTERN. [With a smile.] We have much more important work to do than look at each other's bonnets, Lord Goring.

LORD GORING. Really? What sort of work?

LADY CHILTERN. Oh! dull, useful, delightful things, Factory Acts, Female Inspectors, the Eight Hours' Bill, the Parliamentary

An Ideal Husband

Franchise. . . . Everything, in fact, that you would find thoroughly uninteresting.

LORD GORING. And never bonnets?

LADY CHILTERN. [With mock indignation.] Never bonnets, never!

[LADY CHILTERN goes out through the door leading to her boudoir.]

SIR ROBERT CHILTERN. [Takes LORD GORING'S hand.] You have been a good friend to me, Arthur, a thoroughly good friend.

LORD GORING. I don't know that I have been able to do much for you, Robert, as yet. In fact, I have not been able to do anything for you, as far as I can see. I am thoroughly disappointed with myself.

SIR ROBERT CHILTERN. You have enabled me to tell you the truth. That is something. The truth has always stifled me.

LORD GORING. Ah! the truth is a thing I get rid of as soon as possible! Bad habit, by the way. Makes one very unpopular at the club . . . with the older members. They call it being conceited. Perhaps it is.

SIR ROBERT CHILTERN. I would to God that I had been able to tell the truth . . . to live the truth. Ah! that is the great thing in life, to live the truth. [Sighs, and goes towards the door.] I'll see you soon again, Arthur, shan't I?

LORD GORING. Certainly. Whenever you like. I'm going to look in at the Bachelors' Ball to-night, unless I find something better to do. But I'll come round to-morrow morning. If you should want me to-night by any chance, send round a note to Curzon Street.

SIR ROBERT CHILTERN. Thank you.

[As he reaches the door, LADY CHILTERN enters from her boudoir.]

LADY CHILTERN. You are not going, Robert?

SIR ROBERT CHILTERN. I have some letters to write, dear.

LADY CHILTERN. [Going to him.] You work too hard, Robert. You seem never to think of yourself, and you are looking so tired.

SIR ROBERT CHILTERN. It is nothing, dear, nothing.

[He kisses her and goes out.]

LADY CHILTERN. [To LORD GORING.] Do sit down. I am so glad you have called. I want to talk to you about . . . well, not about bonnets, or the Woman's Liberal Association. You take far too much interest in the first subject, and not nearly enough in the second.

LORD GORING. You want to talk to me about Mrs. Cheveley?

LADY CHILTERN. Yes. You have guessed it. After you left last night I found out that what she had said was really true. Of course I made Robert write her a letter at once, withdrawing his promise.

LORD GORING. So he gave me to understand.

LADY CHILTERN. To have kept it would have been the first stain on a career that has been stainless always. Robert must be above reproach. He is not like other men. He cannot afford to do what other men do. [She looks at LORD GORING, who remains silent.] Don't you agree with me? You are Robert's greatest friend. You are our greatest friend, Lord Goring. No one, except myself, knows Robert better than you do. He has no secrets from me, and I don't think he has any from you.

LORD GORING. He certainly has no secrets from me. At least I don't think so.

LADY CHILTERN. Then am I not right in my estimate of him? I know I am right. But speak to me frankly.

LORD GORING. [Looking straight at her.] Quite frankly?

LADY CHILTERN. Surely. You have nothing to conceal, have you?

LORD GORING. Nothing. But, my dear Lady Chiltern, I think, if you will allow me to say so, that in practical life -

LADY CHILTERN. [Smiling.] Of which you know so little, Lord Goring -

LORD GORING. Of which I know nothing by experience, though I know something by observation. I think that in practical life there is something about success, actual success, that is a little unscrupulous, something about ambition that is unscrupulous always. Once a man has set his heart and soul on getting to a certain point, if he has to climb the crag, he climbs the crag; if he has to walk in the mire -

LADY CHILTERN. Well?

LORD GORING. He walks in the mire. Of course I am only talking generally about life.

LADY CHILTERN. [Gravely.] I hope so. Why do you look at me so strangely, Lord Goring?

LORD GORING. Lady Chiltern, I have sometimes thought that . . . perhaps you are a little hard in some of your views on life. I think that . . . often you don't make sufficient allowances. In every nature there are elements of weakness, or worse than weakness. Supposing, for instance, that - that any public man, my father, or Lord Merton, or Robert, say, had, years ago, written some foolish letter to some one . . .

LADY CHILTERN. What do you mean by a foolish letter?

LORD GORING. A letter gravely compromising one's position. I am only putting an imaginary case.

LADY CHILTERN. Robert is as incapable of doing a foolish thing as he is of doing a wrong thing.

LORD GORING. [After a long pause.] Nobody is incapable of doing a foolish thing. Nobody is incapable of doing a wrong thing.

LADY CHILTERN. Are you a Pessimist? What will the other dandies say? They will all have to go into mourning.

LORD GORING. [Rising.] No, Lady Chiltern, I am not a Pessimist. Indeed I am not sure that I quite know what Pessimism really means. All I do know is that life cannot be understood without much charity, cannot be lived without much charity. It is love, and not German philosophy, that is the true explanation of this world, whatever may be the explanation of the next. And if you are ever in trouble, Lady Chiltern, trust me absolutely, and I will help you in every way I can. If you ever want me, come to me for my assistance, and you shall have it. Come at once to me.

LADY CHILTERN. [Looking at him in surprise.] Lord Goring, you are talking quite seriously. I don't think I ever heard you talk seriously before.

LORD GORING. [Laughing.] You must excuse me, Lady Chiltern. It won't occur again, if I can help it.

LADY CHILTERN. But I like you to be serious.

[Enter MABEL CHILTERN, in the most ravishing frock.]

MABEL CHILTERN. Dear Gertrude, don't say such a dreadful thing to Lord Goring. Seriousness would be very unbecoming to him. Good afternoon Lord Goring! Pray be as trivial as you can.

LORD GORING. I should like to, Miss Mabel, but I am afraid I am . . . a little out of practice this morning; and besides, I have to be going now.

MABEL CHILTERN. Just when I have come in! What dreadful manners you have! I am sure you were very badly brought up.

LORD GORING. I was.

MABEL CHILTERN. I wish I had brought you up!

LORD GORING. I am so sorry you didn't.

MABEL CHILTERN. It is too late now, I suppose

LORD GORING. [Smiling.] I am not so sure.

MABEL CHILTERN. Will you ride to-morrow morning?

LORD GORING. Yes, at ten.

MABEL CHILTERN. Don't forget

LORD GORING. Of course I shan't. By the way, Lady Chiltern, there is no list of your guests in THE MORNING POST of to-day. It has apparently been crowded out by the County Council, or the Lambeth Conference, or something equally boring. Could you let me have a list? I have a particular reason for asking you.

LADY CHILTERN. I am sure Mr. Trafford will be able to give you one.

LORD GORING. Thanks, so much.

MABEL CHILTERN. Tommy is the most useful person in London.

LORD GORING [Turning to her.] And who is the most ornamental?

MABEL CHILTERN [Triumphantly.] I am.

LORD GORING. How clever of you to guess it! [Takes up his hat and cane.] Good-bye, Lady Chiltern! You will remember what I said to you, won't you?

LADY CHILTERN. Yes; but I don't know why you said it to me.

LORD GORING. I hardly know myself. Good-bye, Miss Mabel!

MABEL CHILTERN [With a little moue of disappointment.] I wish you were not going. I have had four wonderful adventures this morning; four and a half, in fact. You might stop and listen to some of them.

LORD GORING. How very selfish of you to have four and a half! There won't be any left for me.

MABEL CHILTERN. I don't want you to have any. They would not be good for you.

LORD GORING. That is the first unkind thing you have ever said to me. How charmingly you said it! Ten to-morrow.

MABEL CHILTERN. Sharp.

LORD GORING. Quite sharp. But don't bring Mr. Trafford.

MABEL CHILTERN. [With a little toss of the head.] Of course I shan't bring Tommy Trafford. Tommy Trafford is in great disgrace.

LORD GORING. I am delighted to hear it. [Bows and goes out.]

MABEL CHILTERN. Gertrude, I wish you would speak to Tommy Trafford.

LADY CHILTERN. What has poor Mr. Trafford done this time? Robert says he is the best secretary he has ever had.

MABEL CHILTERN. Well, Tommy has proposed to me again. Tommy really does nothing but propose to me. He proposed to me last night in the music-room, when I was quite unprotected, as there was an elaborate trio going on. I didn't dare to make the smallest repartee, I need hardly tell you. If I had, it would have stopped the music at once. Musical people are so absurdly unreasonable. They always want one to be perfectly dumb at the very moment when one is longing to be absolutely deaf. Then he proposed to me in broad daylight this morning, in front of that dreadful statue of Achilles. Really, the things that go on in front of that work of art are quite appalling. The police should interfere. At luncheon I saw by the glare in his eye that he was going to propose again, and I just managed to check him in time by assuring him that I was a bimetallist. Fortunately I don't know what bimetallism means. And I don't believe anybody else does either. But the observation crushed Tommy for ten minutes. He looked quite shocked. And then Tommy is so annoying in the way he proposes. If he proposed at the top of his voice, I should not mind so much. That might produce some effect on the public. But he does it in a horrid confidential way. When Tommy wants to be romantic he talks to one just like a doctor. I am very fond of Tommy, but his methods of proposing are quite out of date. I wish, Gertrude, you would speak to him, and tell him that once a week is quite often enough to propose to any one, and that it should always be done in a manner that attracts some attention.

LADY CHILTERN. Dear Mabel, don't talk like that. Besides, Robert thinks very highly of Mr. Trafford. He believes he has a brilliant future before him.

MABEL CHILTERN. Oh! I wouldn't marry a man with a future before him for anything under the sun.

LADY CHILTERN. Mabel!

MABEL CHILTERN. I know, dear. You married a man with a future, didn't you? But then Robert was a genius, and you have a noble, self-sacrificing character. You can stand geniuses. I have no, character at all, and Robert is the only genius I could ever bear. As a rule, I think they are quite impossible. Geniuses talk so much, don't they? Such a bad habit! And they are always thinking about themselves, when I want them to be thinking about me. I must go round now and rehearse at Lady Basildon's. You remember, we are having tableaux, don't you? The Triumph of something, I don't know what! I hope it will be triumph of me. Only triumph I am really interested in at present. [Kisses LADY CHILTERN and goes out; then comes running back.] Oh, Gertrude, do you know who is coming to see you? That dreadful Mrs. Cheveley, in a most lovely gown. Did you ask her?

LADY CHILTERN. [Rising.] Mrs. Cheveley! Coming to see me? Impossible!

MABEL CHILTERN. I assure you she is coming upstairs, as large as life and not nearly so natural.

LADY CHILTERN. You need not wait, Mabel. Remember, Lady Basildon is expecting you.

MABEL CHILTERN. Oh! I must shake hands with Lady Markby. She is delightful. I love being scolded by her.

[Enter MASON.]

MASON. Lady Markby. Mrs. Cheveley.

[Enter LADY MARKBY and MRS. CHEVELEY.]

LADY CHILTERN. [Advancing to meet them.] Dear Lady Markby, how nice of you to come and see me! [Shakes hands with her, and bows somewhat distantly to MRS. CHEVELEY.] Won't you sit down, Mrs. Cheveley?

MRS. CHEVELEY. Thanks. Isn't that Miss Chiltern? I should like so much to know her.

LADY CHILTERN. Mabel, Mrs. Cheveley wishes to know you.

[MABEL CHILTERN gives a little nod.]

MRS. CHEVELEY [Sitting down.] I thought your frock so charming last night, Miss Chiltern. So simple and . . . suitable.

MABEL CHILTERN. Really? I must tell my dressmaker. It will be such a surprise to her. Good-bye, Lady Markby!

LADY MARKBY. Going already?

MABEL CHILTERN. I am so sorry but I am obliged to. I am just off to rehearsal. I have got to stand on my head in some tableaux.

LADY MARKBY. On your head, child? Oh! I hope not. I believe it is most unhealthy. [Takes a seat on the sofa next LADY CHILTERN.]

MABEL CHILTERN. But it is for an excellent charity: in aid of the Undeserving, the only people I am really interested in. I am the secretary, and Tommy Trafford is treasurer.

MRS. CHEVELEY. And what is Lord Goring?

MABEL CHILTERN. Oh! Lord Goring is president.

MRS. CHEVELEY. The post should suit him admirably, unless he has deteriorated since I knew him first.

LADY MARKBY. [Reflecting.] You are remarkably modern, Mabel. A little too modern, perhaps. Nothing is so dangerous as being too modern. One is apt to grow old-fashioned quite suddenly. I have known many instances of it

MABEL CHILTERN. What a dreadful prospect!

LADY MARKBY. Ah! my dear, you need not be nervous. You will always be as pretty as possible. That is the best fashion there is, and the only fashion that England succeeds in setting.

An Ideal Husband

MABEL CHILTERN. [With a curtsey.] Thank you so much, Lady Markby, for England . . . and myself. [Goes out.]

LADY MARKBY. [Turning to LADY CHILTERN.] Dear Gertrude, we just called to know if Mrs. Cheveley's diamond brooch has been found.

LADY CHILTERN. Here?

MRS. CHEVELEY. Yes. I missed it when I got back to Claridge's, and I thought I might possibly have dropped it here.

LADY CHILTERN. I have heard nothing about it. But I will send for the butler and ask. [Touches the bell.]

MRS. CHEVELEY. Oh, pray don't trouble, Lady Chiltern. I dare say I lost it at the Opera, before we came on here.

LADY MARKBY. Ah yes, I suppose it must have been at the Opera. The fact is, we all scramble and jostle so much nowadays that I wonder we have anything at all left on us at the end of an evening. I know myself that, when I am coming back from the Drawing Room, I always feel as if I hadn't a shred on me, except a small shred of decent reputation, just enough to prevent the lower classes making painful observations through the windows of the carriage. The fact is that our Society is terribly over-populated. Really, some one should arrange a proper scheme of assisted emigration. It would do a great deal of good.

MRS. CHEVELEY. I quite agree with you, Lady Markby. It is nearly six years since I have been in London for the Season, and I must say Society has become dreadfully mixed. One sees the oddest people everywhere.

LADY MARKBY. That is quite true, dear. But one needn't know them. I'm sure I don't know half the people who come to my house. Indeed, from all I hear, I shouldn't like to.

[Enter MASON.]

LADY CHILTERN. What sort of a brooch was it that you lost, Mrs. Cheveley?

MRS. CHEVELEY. A diamond snake-brooch with a ruby, a rather large ruby.

LADY MARKBY. I thought you said there was a sapphire on the head, dear?

MRS. CHEVELEY [Smiling.] No, lady Markby - a ruby.

LADY MARKBY. [Nodding her head.] And very becoming, I am quite sure.

LADY CHILTERN. Has a ruby and diamond brooch been found in any of the rooms this morning, Mason?

MASON. No, my lady.

MRS. CHEVELEY. It really is of no consequence, Lady Chiltern. I am so sorry to have put you to any inconvenience.

LADY CHILTERN. [Coldly.] Oh, it has been no inconvenience. That will do, Mason. You can bring tea.

[Exit MASON.]

LADY MARKBY. Well, I must say it is most annoying to lose anything. I remember once at Bath, years ago, losing in the Pump Room an exceedingly handsome cameo bracelet that Sir John had given me. I don't think he has ever given me anything since, I am sorry to say. He has sadly degenerated. Really, this horrid House of Commons quite ruins our husbands for us. I think the Lower House by far the greatest blow to a happy married life that there has been since that terrible thing called the Higher Education of Women was invented.

LADY CHILTERN. Ah! it is heresy to say that in this house, Lady Markby. Robert is a great champion of the Higher Education of Women, and so, I am afraid, am I.

MRS. CHEVELEY. The higher education of men is what I should like to see. Men need it so sadly.

LADY MARKBY. They do, dear. But I am afraid such a scheme would be quite unpractical. I don't think man has much capacity for development. He has got as far as he can, and that is not far, is it? With regard to women, well, dear Gertrude, you belong to the younger generation, and I am sure it is all right if you approve of it. In my time, of course, we were taught not to understand anything. That was the old system, and wonderfully interesting it was. I assure you that the amount of things I and my poor dear sister were taught not to understand was quite extraordinary. But modern women understand everything, I am told.

MRS. CHEVELEY. Except their husbands. That is the one thing the modern woman never understands.

LADY MARKBY. And a very good thing too, dear, I dare say. It might break up many a happy home if they did. Not yours, I need hardly say, Gertrude. You have married a pattern husband. I wish I could say as much for myself. But since Sir John has taken to attending the debates regularly, which he never used to do in the good old days, his language has become quite impossible. He always seems to think that he is addressing the House, and consequently whenever he discusses the state of the agricultural labourer, or the Welsh Church, or something quite improper of that kind, I am obliged to send all the servants out of the room. It is not pleasant to see one's own butler, who has been with one for twenty-three years, actually blushing at the side-board, and the footmen making contortions in corners like persons in circuses. I assure you my life will be quite ruined unless they send John at once to the Upper House. He won't take any interest in politics then, will he? The House of Lords is so sensible. An assembly of gentlemen. But in his present state, Sir John is really a great trial. Why, this morning before breakfast was half over, he stood up on the hearthrug, put his hands in his pockets, and appealed to the country at the top of his voice. I left the table as soon as I had my second cup of tea, I need hardly say. But his violent language could be heard all over the house! I trust, Gertrude, that Sir Robert is not like that

LADY CHILTERN. But I am very much interested in politics, Lady Markby. I love to hear Robert talk about them.

LADY MARKBY. Well, I hope he is not as devoted to Blue Books as Sir John is. I don't think they can be quite improving reading for any one.

MRS. CHEVELEY [Languidly.] I have never read a Blue Book. I prefer books . . . in yellow covers.

LADY MARKBY. [Genially unconscious.] Yellow is a gayer colour, is it not? I used to wear yellow a good deal in my early days, and would do so now if Sir John was not so painfully personal in his observations, and a man on the question of dress is always ridiculous, is he not?

MRS. CHEVELEY. Oh, no! I think men are the only authorities on dress.

LADY MARKBY. Really? One wouldn't say so from the sort of hats they wear? would one?

[The butler enters, followed by the footman. Tea is set on a small table close to LADY CHILTERN.]

LADY CHILTERN. May I give you some tea, Mrs. Cheveley?

MRS. CHEVELEY. Thanks. [The butler hands MRS. CHEVELEY a cup of tea on a salver.]

LADY CHILTERN. Some tea, Lady Markby?

LADY MARKBY. No thanks, dear. [The servants go out.] The fact is, I have promised to go round for ten minutes to see poor Lady Brancaster, who is in very great trouble. Her daughter, quite a well-brought-up girl, too, has actually become engaged to be married to a curate in Shropshire. It is very sad, very sad indeed. I can't understand this modern mania for curates. In my time we girls saw them, of course, running about the place like rabbits. But we never took any notice of them, I need hardly say. But I am told that nowadays country society is quite honeycombed with them. I think it most irreligious. And then the eldest son has quarrelled with his father, and it is said that when they meet at the club Lord Brancaster always hides himself behind the money article in THE TIMES. However, I believe that is quite a common occurrence nowadays and that they have to take in extra copies of THE TIMES at all the clubs in St. James's Street; there are so many sons who won't have anything to do with their fathers, and so many fathers who won't speak to their sons. I think myself, it is very much to be regretted.

MRS. CHEVELEY. So do I. Fathers have so much to learn from their sons nowadays.

LADY MARKBY. Really, dear? What?

MRS. CHEVELEY. The art of living. The only really Fine Art we have produced in modern times.

LADY MARKBY. [Shaking her head.] Ah! I am afraid Lord Brancaster knew a good deal about that. More than his poor wife ever did. [Turning to LADY CHILTERN.] You know Lady Brancaster, don't you, dear?

LADY CHILTERN. Just slightly. She was staying at Langton last autumn, when we were there.

LADY MARKBY. Well, like all stout women, she looks the very picture of happiness, as no doubt you noticed. But there are many tragedies in her family, besides this affair of the curate. Her own sister, Mrs. Jekyll, had a most unhappy life; through no fault of her own, I am sorry to say. She ultimately was so broken-hearted that she went into a convent, or on to the operatic stage, I forget which. No; I think it was decorative art-needlework she took up. I know she had lost all sense of pleasure in life. [Rising.] And now, Gertrude, if you will allow me, I shall leave Mrs. Cheveley in your charge and call back for her in a quarter of an hour. Or perhaps, dear Mrs. Cheveley, you wouldn't mind waiting in the carriage while I am with Lady Brancaster. As I intend it to be a visit of condolence, I shan't stay long.

MRS. CHEVELEY [Rising.] I don't mind waiting in the carriage at all, provided there is somebody to look at one.

LADY MARKBY. Well, I hear the curate is always prowling about the house.

MRS. CHEVELEY. I am afraid I am not fond of girl friends.

LADY CHILTERN [Rising.] Oh, I hope Mrs. Cheveley will stay here a little. I should like to have a few minutes' conversation with her.

MRS. CHEVELEY. How very kind of you, Lady Chiltern! Believe me, nothing would give me greater pleasure.

LADY MARKBY. Ah! no doubt you both have many pleasant reminiscences of your schooldays to talk over together. Good-bye, dear Gertrude! Shall I see you at Lady Bonar's to-night? She has discovered a wonderful new genius. He does . . . nothing at all, I believe. That is a great comfort, is it not?

LADY CHILTERN. Robert and I are dining at home by ourselves to-night, and I don't think I shall go anywhere afterwards. Robert, of course, will have to be in the House. But there is nothing interesting on.

LADY MARKBY. Dining at home by yourselves? Is that quite prudent? Ah, I forgot, your husband is an exception. Mine is the general rule, and nothing ages a woman so rapidly as having married the general rule. [Exit LADY MARKBY.]

MRS. CHEVELEY. Wonderful woman, Lady Markby, isn't she? Talks more and says less than anybody I ever met. She is made to be a public speaker. Much more so than her husband, though he is a typical Englishman, always dull and usually violent.

LADY CHILTERN. [Makes no answer, but remains standing. There is a pause. Then the eyes of the two women meet. LADY CHILTERN looks stern and pale. MRS. CHEVELEY seem rather amused.] Mrs. Cheveley, I think it is right to tell you quite frankly that, had I known who you really were, I should not have invited you to my house last night.

MRS. CHEVELEY [With an impertinent smile.] Really?

LADY CHILTERN. I could not have done so.

MRS. CHEVELEY. I see that after all these years you have not changed a bit, Gertrude.

LADY CHILTERN. I never change.

MRS. CHEVELEY [Elevating her eyebrows.] Then life has taught you nothing?

LADY CHILTERN. It has taught me that a person who has once been guilty of a dishonest and dishonourable action may be guilty of it a second time, and should be shunned.

MRS. CHEVELEY. Would you apply that rule to every one?

LADY CHILTERN. Yes, to every one, without exception.

MRS. CHEVELEY. Then I am sorry for you, Gertrude, very sorry for you.

LADY CHILTERN. You see now, I was sure, that for many reasons any further acquaintance between us during your stay in London is quite impossible?

MRS. CHEVELEY [Leaning back in her chair.] Do you know, Gertrude, I don't mind your talking morality a bit. Morality is simply the attitude we adopt towards people whom we personally dislike. You dislike me. I am quite aware of that. And I have always detested you. And yet I have come here to do you a service.

LADY CHILTERN. [Contemptuously.] Like the service you wished to render my husband last night, I suppose. Thank heaven, I saved him from that.

MRS. CHEVELEY. [Starting to her feet.] It was you who made him write that insolent letter to me? It was you who made him break his promise?

LADY CHILTERN. Yes.

MRS. CHEVELEY. Then you must make him keep it. I give you till to- morrow morning - no more. If by that time your husband does not solemnly bind himself to help me in this great scheme in which I am interested -

LADY CHILTERN. This fraudulent speculation -

MRS. CHEVELEY. Call it what you choose. I hold your husband in the hollow of my hand, and if you are wise you will make him do what I tell him.

LADY CHILTERN. [Rising and going towards her.] You are impertinent. What has my husband to do with you? With a woman like you?

MRS. CHEVELEY [With a bitter laugh.] In this world like meets with like. It is because your husband is himself fraudulent and dishonest that we pair so well together. Between you and him there are chasms. He and I are closer than friends. We are enemies linked together. The same sin binds us.

LADY CHILTERN. How dare you class my husband with yourself? How dare you threaten him or me? Leave my house. You are unfit to enter it.

[SIR ROBERT CHILTERN enters from behind. He hears his wife's last words, and sees to whom they are addressed. He grows deadly pale.]

MRS. CHEVELEY. Your house! A house bought with the price of dishonour. A house, everything in which has been paid for by fraud. [Turns round and sees SIR ROBERT CHILTERN.] Ask him what the origin of his fortune is! Get him to tell you how he sold to a stockbroker a Cabinet secret. Learn from him to what you owe your position.

LADY CHILTERN. It is not true! Robert! It is not true!

MRS. CHEVELEY. [Pointing at him with outstretched finger.] Look at him! Can he deny it? Does he dare to?

SIR ROBERT CHILTERN. Go! Go at once. You have done your worst now.

MRS. CHEVELEY. My worst? I have not yet finished with you, with either of you. I give you both till to-morrow at noon. If by then you don't do what I bid you to do, the whole world shall know the origin of Robert Chiltern.

[SIR ROBERT CHILTERN strikes the bell. Enter MASON.]

SIR ROBERT CHILTERN. Show Mrs. Cheveley out.

[MRS. CHEVELEY starts; then bows with somewhat exaggerated politeness to LADY CHILTERN, who makes no sign of response. As she passes by SIR ROBERT CHILTERN, who is standing close to the door, she pauses for a moment and looks him straight in the face. She then goes out, followed by the servant, who closes the door after him. The husband and wife are left alone. LADY CHILTERN stands like some one in a dreadful dream. Then she turns round and looks at her husband. She looks at him with strange eyes, as though she were seeing him for the first time.]

LADY CHILTERN. You sold a Cabinet secret for money! You began your life with fraud! You built up your career on dishonour! Oh, tell me it is not true! Lie to me! Lie to me! Tell me it is not true!

SIR ROBERT CHILTERN. What this woman said is quite true. But, Gertrude, listen to me. You don't realise how I was tempted. Let me tell you the whole thing. [Goes towards her.]

LADY CHILTERN. Don't come near me. Don't touch me. I feel as if you had soiled me for ever. Oh! what a mask you have been wearing all these years! A horrible painted mask! You sold yourself for money. Oh! a common thief were better. You put yourself up to sale to the highest bidder! You were bought in the market. You lied to the whole world. And yet you will not lie to me.

SIR ROBERT CHILTERN. [Rushing towards her.] Gertrude! Gertrude!

LADY CHILTERN. [Thrusting him back with outstretched hands.] No, don't speak! Say nothing! Your voice wakes terrible memories - memories of things that made me love you - memories of words that made me love you - memories that now are horrible to me. And how I worshipped you! You were to me something apart from common life, a thing pure, noble, honest, without stain. The world seemed to me finer because you were in it, and goodness more real because you lived. And now - oh, when I think that I made of a man like you my ideal! the ideal of my life!

SIR ROBERT CHILTERN. There was your mistake. There was your error. The error all women commit. Why can't you women love us, faults and all? Why do you place us on monstrous pedestals? We have all feet of clay, women as well as men; but when we men love women, we love them knowing their weaknesses, their follies, their imperfections, love them all the more, it may be, for that reason. It is not the perfect, but the imperfect, who have need of love. It is when we are wounded by our own hands, or by the hands of others, that love should come to cure us - else what use is love at all? All sins, except a sin against itself, Love should forgive. All lives, save loveless lives, true Love should pardon. A man's love is like that. It is wider, larger, more human than a woman's. Women think that they are making ideals of men. What they are making of us are false idols merely. You made your false idol of me, and I had not the courage to come down, show you my wounds, tell you my weaknesses. I was afraid that I might lose your love, as I have lost it now. And so, last night you ruined my life for me - yes, ruined it! What this woman asked of me was nothing compared to what she offered to me. She offered security, peace, stability. The sin of my youth, that I had thought was buried, rose up in front of me, hideous, horrible, with its hands at my throat. I could have killed it for ever, sent it back into its tomb, destroyed its record, burned the one witness against me. You prevented me. No one but you, you know it. And now what is there before me but public disgrace, ruin, terrible shame, the mockery of the world, a lonely dishonoured life, a lonely dishonoured death, it may be, some day? Let women make no more ideals of men! let them not put them on alters and bow before them, or they may ruin other lives as completely as you - you whom I have so wildly loved - have ruined mine!

[He passes from the room. LADY CHILTERN rushes towards him, but the door is closed when she reaches it. Pale with anguish, bewildered, helpless, she sways like a plant in the water. Her hands, outstretched, stem to tremble in the air like blossoms in the mind. Then she flings herself down beside a sofa and buries her face. Her sobs are like the sobs of a child.]

ACT DROP

THIRD ACT

SCENE

The Library in Lord Goring's house. An Adam room. On the right is the door leading into the hall. On the left, the door of the smoking-room. A pair of folding doors at the back open into the drawing-room. The fire is lit. Phipps, the butler, is arranging some newspapers on the writing-table. The distinction of Phipps is his impassivity. He has been termed by enthusiasts the Ideal Butler. The Sphinx is not so incommunicable. He is a mask with a manner. Of his intellectual or emotional life, history knows nothing. He represents the dominance of form.

[Enter LORD GORING in evening dress with a buttonhole. He is wearing a silk hat and Inverness cape. White-gloved, he carries a Louis Seize cane. His are all the delicate fopperies of Fashion. One sees that he stands in immediate relation to modern life, makes it indeed, and so masters it. He is the first well-dressed philosopher in the history of thought.]

LORD GORING. Got my second buttonhole for me, Phipps? *dandy*

PHIPPS. Yes, my lord. [Takes his hat, cane, and cape, and presents new buttonhole on salver.]

LORD GORING. Rather distinguished thing, Phipps. I am the only person of the smallest importance in London at present who wears a buttonhole.

PHIPPS. Yes, my lord. I have observed that,

LORD GORING. [Taking out old buttonhole.] You see, Phipps, Fashion is what one wears oneself. What is unfashionable is what other people wear.

PHIPPS. Yes, my lord.

LORD GORING. Just as vulgarity is simply the conduct of other people.

PHIPPS. Yes, my lord.

LORD GORING. [Putting in a new buttonhole.] And falsehoods the truths of other people.

PHIPPS. Yes, my lord.

LORD GORING. Other people are quite dreadful. The only possible society is oneself.

PHIPPS. Yes, my lord.

LORD GORING. To love oneself is the beginning of a lifelong romance, Phipps.

PHIPPS. Yes, my lord.

LORD GORING. [Looking at himself in the glass.] Don't think I quite like this buttonhole, Phipps. Makes me look a little too old. Makes me almost in the prime of life, eh, Phipps?

PHIPPS. I don't observe any alteration in your lordship's appearance.

LORD GORING. You don't, Phipps?

PHIPPS. No, my lord.

LORD GORING. I am not quite sure. For the future a more trivial buttonhole, Phipps, on Thursday evenings.

PHIPPS. I will speak to the florist, my lord. She has had a loss in her family lately, which perhaps accounts for the lack of triviality your lordship complains of in the buttonhole.

LORD GORING. Extraordinary thing about the lower classes in England - they are always losing their relations.

PHIPPS. Yes, my lord! They are extremely fortunate in that respect.

LORD GORING. [Turns round and looks at him. PHIPPS remains impassive.] Hum! Any letters, Phipps?

PHIPPS. Three, my lord. [Hands letters on a salver.]

LORD GORING. [Takes letters.] Want my cab round in twenty minutes.

PHIPPS. Yes, my lord. [Goes towards door.]

LORD GORING. [Holds up letter in pink envelope.] Ahem! Phipps, when did this letter arrive?

PHIPPS. It was brought by hand just after your lordship went to the club.

LORD GORING. That will do. [Exit PHIPPS.] Lady Chiltern's handwriting on Lady Chiltern's pink notepaper. That is rather curious. I thought Robert was to write. Wonder what Lady Chiltern has got to say to me? [Sits at bureau and opens letter, and reads it.] 'I want you. I trust you. I am coming to you. Gertrude.' [Puts down the letter with a puzzled look. Then takes it up, and reads it again slowly.] 'I want you. I trust you. I am coming to you.' So she has found out everything! Poor woman! Poor woman! [Pulls out watch and looks at it.] But what an hour to call! Ten o'clock! I shall have to give up going to the Berkshires. However, it is always nice to be expected, and not to arrive. I am not expected at the Bachelors', so I shall certainly go there. Well, I will make her stand by her husband. That is the only thing for her to do. That is the only thing for any woman to do. It is the growth of the moral sense in women that makes marriage such a hopeless, one- sided institution. Ten o'clock. She should be here soon. I must tell Phipps I am not in to any one else. [Goes towards bell]

[Enter PHIPPS.]

PHIPPS. Lord Caversham.

LORD GORING. Oh, why will parents always appear at the wrong time? Some extraordinary mistake in nature, I suppose. [Enter LORD CAVERSHAM.] Delighted to see you, my dear father. [Goes to meet him.]

LORD CAVERSHAM. Take my cloak off.

LORD GORING. Is it worth while, father?

LORD CAVERSHAM. Of course it is worth while, sir. Which is the most comfortable chair?

LORD GORING. This one, father. It is the chair I use myself, when I have visitors.

LORD CAVERSHAM. Thank ye. No draught, I hope, in this room?

LORD GORING. No, father.

LORD CAVERSHAM. [Sitting down.] Glad to hear it. Can't stand draughts. No draughts at home.

LORD GORING. Good many breezes, father.

LORD CAVERSHAM. Eh? Eh? Don't understand what you mean. Want to have a serious conversation with you, sir.

LORD GORING. My dear father! At this hour?

LORD CAVERSHAM. Well, sir, it is only ten o'clock. What is your objection to the hour? I think the hour is an admirable hour!

LORD GORING. Well, the fact is, father, this is not my day for talking seriously. I am very sorry, but it is not my day.

LORD CAVERSHAM. What do you mean, sir?

LORD GORING. During the Season, father, I only talk seriously on the first Tuesday in every month, from four to seven.

LORD CAVERSHAM. Well, make it Tuesday, sir, make it Tuesday.

LORD GORING. But it is after seven, father, and my doctor says I must not have any serious conversation after seven. It makes me talk in my sleep.

LORD CAVERSHAM. Talk in your sleep, sir? What does that matter? You are not married.

LORD GORING. No, father, I am not married.

An Ideal Husband

LORD CAVERSHAM. Hum! That is what I have come to talk to you about, sir. You have got to get married, and at once. Why, when I was your age, sir, I had been an inconsolable widower for three months, and was already paying my addresses to your admirable mother. Damme, sir, it is your duty to get married. You can't be always living for pleasure. Every man of position is married nowadays. Bachelors are not fashionable any more. They are a damaged lot. Too much is known about them. You must get a wife, sir. Look where your friend Robert Chiltern has got to by probity, hard work, and a sensible marriage with a good woman. Why don't you imitate him, sir? Why don't you take him for your model?

LORD GORING. I think I shall, father.

LORD CAVERSHAM. I wish you would, sir. Then I should be happy. At present I make your mother's life miserable on your account. You are heartless, sir, quite heartless

LORD GORING. I hope not, father.

LORD CAVERSHAM. And it is high time for you to get married. You are thirty-four years of age, sir.

LORD GORING. Yes, father, but I only admit to thirty-two - thirty-one and a half when I have a really good buttonhole. This buttonhole is not . . . trivial enough.

LORD CAVERSHAM. I tell you you are thirty-four, sir. And there is a draught in your room, besides, which makes your conduct worse. Why did you tell me there was no draught, sir? I feel a draught, sir, I feel it distinctly.

LORD GORING. So do I, father. It is a dreadful draught. I will come and see you to-morrow, father. We can talk over anything you like. Let me help you on with your cloak, father.

LORD CAVERSHAM. No, sir; I have called this evening for a definite purpose, and I am going to see it through at all costs to my health or yours. Put down my cloak, sir.

LORD GORING. Certainly, father. But let us go into another room. [Rings bell.] There is a dreadful draught here. [Enter PHIPPS.] Phipps, is there a good fire in the smoking-room?

PHIPPS. Yes, my lord.

LORD GORING. Come in there, father. Your sneezes are quite heartrending.

LORD CAVERSHAM. Well, sir, I suppose I have a right to sneeze when I choose?

LORD GORING. [Apologetically.] Quite so, father. I was merely expressing sympathy.

LORD CAVERSHAM. Oh, damn sympathy. There is a great deal too much of that sort of thing going on nowadays.

LORD GORING. I quite agree with you, father. If there was less sympathy in the world there would be less trouble in the world.

LORD CAVERSHAM. [Going towards the smoking-room.] That is a paradox, sir. I hate paradoxes.

LORD GORING. So do I, father. Everybody one meets is a paradox nowadays. It is a great bore. It makes society so obvious.

LORD CAVERSHAM. [Turning round, and looking at his son beneath his bushy eyebrows.] Do you always really understand what you say, sir?

LORD GORING. [After some hesitation.] Yes, father, if I listen attentively.

LORD CAVERSHAM. [Indignantly.] If you listen attentively! . . . Conceited young puppy!

[Goes off grumbling into the smoking-room. PHIPPS enters.]

LORD GORING. Phipps, there is a lady coming to see me this evening on particular business. Show her into the drawing-room when she arrives. You understand?

PHIPPS. Yes, my lord.

LORD GORING. It is a matter of the gravest importance, Phipps.

PHIPPS. I understand, my lord.

LORD GORING. No one else is to be admitted, under any circumstances.

PHIPPS. I understand, my lord. [Bell rings.]

LORD GORING. Ah! that is probably the lady. I shall see her myself.

[Just as he is going towards the door LORD CAVERSHAM enters from the smoking-room.]

LORD CAVERSHAM. Well, sir? am I to wait attendance on you?

LORD GORING. [Considerably perplexed.] In a moment, father. Do excuse me. [LORD CAVERSHAM goes back.] Well, remember my instructions, Phipps - into that room.

PHIPPS. Yes, my lord.

[LORD GORING goes into the smoking-room. HAROLD, the footman shows MRS. CHEVELEY in. Lamia-like, she is in green and silver. She has a cloak of black satin, lined with dead rose-leaf silk.]

HAROLD. What name, madam?

MRS. CHEVELEY. [To PHIPPS, who advances towards her.] Is Lord Goring not here? I was told he was at home?

PHIPPS. His lordship is engaged at present with Lord Caversham, madam.

[Turns a cold, glassy eye on HAROLD, who at once retires.]

MRS. CHEVELEY. [To herself.] How very filial!

PHIPPS. His lordship told me to ask you, madam, to be kind enough to wait in the drawing-room for him. His lordship will come to you there.

MRS. CHEVELEY. [With a look of surprise.] Lord Goring expects me?

PHIPPS. Yes, madam.

MRS. CHEVELEY. Are you quite sure?

PHIPPS. His lordship told me that if a lady called I was to ask her to wait in the drawing-room. [Goes to the door of the drawing-room and opens it.] His lordship's directions on the subject were very precise.

MRS. CHEVELEY. [To herself] How thoughtful of him! To expect the unexpected shows a thoroughly modern intellect. [Goes towards the drawing-room and looks in.] Ugh! How dreary a bachelor's drawing- room always looks. I shall have to alter all this. [PHIPPS brings the lamp from the writing-table.] No, I don't care for that lamp. It is far too glaring. Light some candles.

PHIPPS. [Replaces lamp.] Certainly, madam.

MRS. CHEVELEY. I hope the candles have very becoming shades.

PHIPPS. We have had no complaints about them, madam, as yet.

[Passes into the drawing-room and begins to light the candles.]

MRS. CHEVELEY. [To herself.] I wonder what woman he is waiting for to-night. It will be delightful to catch him. Men always look so silly when they are caught. And they are always being caught. [Looks about room and approaches the writing-table.] What a very interesting room! What a very interesting picture! Wonder what his correspondence is like. [Takes up letters.] Oh, what a very uninteresting correspondence! Bills and cards, debts and dowagers! Who on earth writes to him on pink paper? How silly to write on pink paper! It looks like the beginning of a middle-class romance. Romance should never begin with sentiment. It should begin with science and end with a settlement. [Puts letter down, then takes it up again.] I know that handwriting. That is Gertrude Chiltern's. I remember it perfectly. The ten commandments in every stroke of the pen, and the moral law all over the page. Wonder what Gertrude is writing to him about? Something horrid about me, I suppose. How I detest that woman! [Reads it.] 'I trust you. I want you. I am coming to you. Gertrude.' 'I trust you. I want you. I am coming to you.'

[A look of triumph comes over her face. She is just about to steal the letter, when PHIPPS comes in.]

PHIPPS. The candles in the drawing-room are lit, madam, as you directed.

MRS. CHEVELEY. Thank you. [Rises hastily and slips the letter under a large silver-cased blotting-book that is lying on the table.]

PHIPPS. I trust the shades will be to your liking, madam. They are the most becoming we have. They are the same as his lordship uses himself when he is dressing for dinner.

MRS. CHEVELEY. [With a smile.] Then I am sure they will be perfectly right.

PHIPPS. [Gravely.] Thank you, madam.

[MRS. CHEVELEY goes into the drawing-room. PHIPPS closes the door and retires. The door is then slowly opened, and MRS. CHEVELEY comes out and creeps stealthily towards the writing-table. Suddenly voices are heard from the smoking-room. MRS. CHEVELEY grows pale, and stops. The voices grow louder, and she goes back into the drawing- room, biting her lip.]

[Enter LORD GORING and LORD CAVERSHAM.]

LORD GORING. [Expostulating.] My dear father, if I am to get married, surely you will allow me to choose the time, place, and person? Particularly the person.

LORD CAVERSHAM. [Testily.] That is a matter for me, sir. You would probably make a very poor choice. It is I who should be consulted, not you. There is property at stake. It is not a matter for affection. Affection comes later on in married life.

LORD GORING. Yes. In married life affection comes when people thoroughly dislike each other, father, doesn't it? [Puts on LORD CAVERSHAM'S cloak for him.]

LORD CAVERSHAM. Certainly, sir. I mean certainly not, air. You are talking very foolishly to-night. What I say is that marriage is a matter for common sense.

LORD GORING. But women who have common sense are so curiously plain, father, aren't they? Of course I only speak from hearsay.

LORD CAVERSHAM. No woman, plain or pretty, has any common sense at all, sir. Common sense is the privilege of our sex.

LORD GORING. Quite so. And we men are so self-sacrificing that we never use it, do we, father?

LORD CAVERSHAM. I use it, sir. I use nothing else.

LORD GORING. So my mother tells me.

LORD CAVERSHAM. It is the secret of your mother's happiness. You are very heartless, sir, very heartless.

LORD GORING. I hope not, father.

[Goes out for a moment. Then returns, looking rather put out, with SIR ROBERT CHILTERN.]

SIR ROBERT CHILTERN. My dear Arthur, what a piece of good luck meeting you on the doorstep! Your servant had just told me you were not at home. How extraordinary!

LORD GORING. The fact is, I am horribly busy to-night, Robert, and I gave orders I was not at home to any one. Even my father had a comparatively cold reception. He complained of a draught the whole time.

SIR ROBERT CHILTERN. Ah! you must be at home to me, Arthur. You are my best friend. Perhaps by to-morrow you will be my only friend. My wife has discovered everything.

LORD GORING. Ah! I guessed as much!

SIR ROBERT CHILTERN. [Looking at him.] Really! How?

LORD GORING. [After some hesitation.] Oh, merely by something in the expression of your face as you came in. Who told her?

SIR ROBERT CHILTERN. Mrs. Cheveley herself. And the woman I love knows that I began my career with an act of low dishonesty, that I built up my life upon sands of shame - that I sold, like a common huckster, the secret that had been intrusted to me as a man of honour. I thank heaven poor Lord Radley died without knowing that I betrayed him. I would to God I had died before I had been so horribly tempted, or had fallen so low. [Burying his face in his hands.]

LORD GORING. [After a pause.] You have heard nothing from Vienna yet, in answer to your wire?

SIR ROBERT CHILTERN. [Looking up.] Yes; I got a telegram from the first secretary at eight o'clock to-night.

LORD GORING. Well?

SIR ROBERT CHILTERN. Nothing is absolutely known against her. On the contrary, she occupies a rather high position in society. It is a sort of open secret that Baron Arnheim left her the greater portion of his immense fortune. Beyond that I can learn nothing.

LORD GORING. She doesn't turn out to be a spy, then?

SIR ROBERT CHILTERN. Oh! spies are of no use nowadays. Their profession is over. The newspapers do their work instead.

LORD GORING. And thunderingly well they do it.

SIR ROBERT CHILTERN. Arthur, I am parched with thirst. May I ring for something? Some hock and seltzer?

LORD GORING. Certainly. Let me. [Rings the bell.]

SIR ROBERT CHILTERN. Thanks! I don't know what to do, Arthur, I don't know what to do, and you are my only friend. But what a friend you are - the one friend I can trust. I can trust you absolutely, can't I?

[Enter PHIPPS.]

LORD GORING. My dear Robert, of course. Oh! [To PHIPPS.] Bring some hock and seltzer.

PHIPPS. Yes, my lord.

LORD GORING. And Phipps!

PHIPPS. Yes, my lord.

LORD GORING. Will you excuse me for a moment, Robert? I want to give some directions to my servant.

SIR ROBERT CHILTERN. Certainly.

LORD GORING. When that lady calls, tell her that I am not expected home this evening. Tell her that I have been suddenly called out of town. You understand?

PHIPPS. The lady is in that room, my lord. You told me to show her into that room, my lord.

LORD GORING. You did perfectly right. [Exit PHIPPS.] What a mess I am in. No; I think I shall get through it. I'll give her a lecture through the door. Awkward thing to manage, though.

SIR ROBERT CHILTERN. Arthur, tell me what I should do. My life seems to have crumbled about me. I am a ship without a rudder in a night without a star.

LORD GORING. Robert, you love your wife, don't you?

SIR ROBERT CHILTERN. I love her more than anything in the world. I used to think ambition the great thing. It is not. Love is the great thing in the world. There is nothing but love, and I love her. But I am defamed in her eyes. I am ignoble in her eyes. There is a wide gulf between us now. She has found me out, Arthur, she has found me out.

LORD GORING. Has she never in her life done some folly - some indiscretion - that she should not forgive your sin?

SIR ROBERT CHILTERN. My wife! Never! She does not know what weakness or temptation is. I am of clay like other men. She stands apart as good women do - pitiless in her perfection - cold and stern and without mercy. But I love her, Arthur. We are childless, and I have no one else to love, no one else to love me. Perhaps if God had sent us children she might have been kinder to me. But God has given us a lonely house. And she has cut my heart in two. Don't let us talk of it. I was brutal to her this evening. But I suppose when sinners talk to saints they are brutal always. I said to her things that were hideously true, on my side, from my stand-point, from the standpoint of men. But don't let us talk of that

LORD GORING. Your wife will forgive you. Perhaps at this moment she is forgiving you. She loves you, Robert. Why should she not forgive?

SIR ROBERT CHILTERN. God grant it! God grant it! [Buries his face in his hands.] But there is something more I have to tell you, Arthur.

[Enter PHIPPS with drinks.]

PHIPPS. [Hands hock and seltzer to SIR ROBERT CHILTERN.] Hock and seltzer, sir.

SIR ROBERT CHILTERN. Thank you.

LORD GORING. Is your carriage here, Robert?

SIR ROBERT CHILTERN. No; I walked from the club.

LORD GORING. Sir Robert will take my cab, Phipps.

PHIPPS. Yes, my lord. [Exit.]

LORD GORING. Robert, you don't mind my sending you away?

SIR ROBERT CHILTERN. Arthur, you must let me stay for five minutes. I have made up my mind what I am going to do to-night in the House. The debate on the Argentine Canal is to begin at eleven. [A chair falls in the drawing-room.] What is that?

LORD GORING. Nothing.

SIR ROBERT CHILTERN. I heard a chair fall in the next room. Some one has been listening.

LORD GORING. No, no; there is no one there.

SIR ROBERT CHILTERN. There is some one. There are lights in the room, and the door is ajar. Some one has been listening to every secret of my life. Arthur, what does this mean?

LORD GORING. Robert, you are excited, unnerved. I tell you there is no one in that room. Sit down, Robert.

SIR ROBERT CHILTERN. Do you give me your word that there is no one there?

LORD GORING. Yes.

SIR ROBERT CHILTERN. Your word of honour? [Sits down.]

LORD GORING. Yes.

SIR ROBERT CHILTERN. [Rises.] Arthur, let me see for myself.

LORD GORING. No, no.

SIR ROBERT CHILTERN. If there is no one there why should I not look in that room? Arthur, you must let me go into that room and satisfy myself. Let me know that no eavesdropper has heard my life's secret. Arthur, you don't realise what I am going through.

LORD GORING. Robert, this must stop. I have told you that there is no one in that room - that is enough.

SIR ROBERT CHILTERN. [Rushes to the door of the room.] It is not enough. I insist on going into this room. You have told me there is no one there, so what reason can you have for refusing me?

LORD GORING. For God's sake, don't! There is some one there. Some one whom you must not see.

SIR ROBERT CHILTERN. Ah, I thought so!

LORD GORING. I forbid you to enter that room.

SIR ROBERT CHILTERN. Stand back. My life is at stake. An[
care who is there. I will know who it is to whom I have
secret and my shame. [Enters room.]

LORD GORING. Great heavens! his own wife!

[SIR ROBERT CHILTERN comes back, with a look of scorn and
anger on his face.]

SIR ROBERT CHILTERN. What explanation have you to give me for
the presence of that woman here?

LORD GORING. Robert, I swear to you on my honour that that lady
is stainless and guiltless of all offence towards you.

SIR ROBERT CHILTERN. She is a vile, an infamous thing!

LORD GORING. Don't say that, Robert! It was for your sake she
came here. It was to try and save you she came here. She loves you
and no one else.

SIR ROBERT CHILTERN. You are mad. What have I to do with her
intrigues with you? Let her remain your mistress! You are well
suited to each other. She, corrupt and shameful - you, false as a
friend, treacherous as an enemy even -

LORD GORING. It is not true, Robert. Before heaven, it is not true.
In her presence and in yours I will explain all.

SIR ROBERT CHILTERN. Let me pass, sir. You have lied enough
upon your word of honour.

[SIR ROBERT CHILTERN goes out. LORD GORING rushes to the
door of the drawing-room, when MRS. CHEVELEY comes out,
looking radiant and much amused.]

MRS. CHEVELEY. [With a mock curtsey] Good evening, Lord
Goring!

LORD GORING. Mrs. Cheveley! Great heavens! . . . May I ask what
you were doing in my drawing-room?

MRS. CHEVELEY. Merely listening. I have a perfect passion for listening through keyholes. One always hears such wonderful things through them.

LORD GORING. Doesn't that sound rather like tempting Providence?

MRS. CHEVELEY. Oh! surely Providence can resist temptation by this time. [Makes a sign to him to take her cloak off, which he does.]

LORD GORING. I am glad you have called. I am going to give you some good advice.

MRS. CHEVELEY. Oh! pray don't. One should never give a woman anything that she can't wear in the evening.

LORD GORING. I see you are quite as wilful as you used to be.

MRS. CHEVELEY. Far more! I have greatly improved. I have had more experience.

LORD GORING. Too much experience is a dangerous thing. Pray have a cigarette. Half the pretty women in London smoke cigarettes. Personally I prefer the other half.

MRS. CHEVELEY. Thanks. I never smoke. My dressmaker wouldn't like it, and a woman's first duty in life is to her dressmaker, isn't it? What the second duty is, no one has as yet discovered.

LORD GORING. You have come here to sell me Robert Chiltern's letter, haven't you?

MRS. CHEVELEY. To offer it to you on conditions. How did you guess that?

LORD GORING. Because you haven't mentioned the subject. Have you got it with you?

MRS. CHEVELEY. [Sitting down.] Oh, no! A well-made dress has no pockets.

LORD GORING. What is your price for it?

MRS. CHEVELEY. How absurdly English you are! The English think that a cheque-book can solve every problem in life. Why, my dear Arthur, I have very much more money than you have, and quite as much as Robert Chiltern has got hold of. Money is not what I want.

LORD GORING. What do you want then, Mrs. Cheveley?

MRS. CHEVELEY. Why don't you call me Laura?

LORD GORING. I don't like the name.

MRS. CHEVELEY. You used to adore it.

LORD GORING. Yes: that's why. [MRS. CHEVELEY motions to him to sit down beside her. He smiles, and does so.]

MRS. CHEVELEY. Arthur, you loved me once.

LORD GORING. Yes.

MRS. CHEVELEY. And you asked me to be your wife.

LORD GORING. That was the natural result of my loving you.

MRS. CHEVELEY. And you threw me over because you saw, or said you saw, poor old Lord Mortlake trying to have a violent flirtation with me in the conservatory at Tenby.

LORD GORING. I am under the impression that my lawyer settled that matter with you on certain terms . . . dictated by yourself.

MRS. CHEVELEY. At that time I was poor; you were rich.

LORD GORING. Quite so. That is why you pretended to love me.

MRS. CHEVELEY. [Shrugging her shoulders.] Poor old Lord Mortlake, who had only two topics of conversation, his gout and his wife! I never could quite make out which of the two he was talking about. He used the most horrible language about them both. Well, you were silly, Arthur. Why, Lord Mortlake was never anything more to me than an amusement. One of those utterly tedious amusements one only finds at an English country house on an

English country Sunday. I don't think any one at all morally responsible for what he or she does at an English country house.

LORD GORING. Yes. I know lots of people think that.

MRS. CHEVELEY. I loved you, Arthur.

LORD GORING. My dear Mrs. Cheveley, you have always been far too clever to know anything about love.

MRS. CHEVELEY. I did love you. And you loved me. You know you loved me; and love is a very wonderful thing. I suppose that when a man has once loved a woman, he will do anything for her, except continue to love her? [Puts her hand on his.]

LORD GORING. [Taking his hand away quietly.] Yes: except that.

MRS. CHEVELEY. [After a pause.] I am tired of living abroad. I want to come back to London. I want to have a charming house here. I want to have a salon. If one could only teach the English how to talk, and the Irish how to listen, society here would be quite civilised. Besides, I have arrived at the romantic stage. When I saw you last night at the Chilterns', I knew you were the only person I had ever cared for, if I ever have cared for anybody, Arthur. And so, on the morning of the day you marry me, I will give you Robert Chiltern's letter. That is my offer. I will give it to you now, if you promise to marry me.

LORD GORING. Now?

MRS. CHEVELEY. [Smiling.] To-morrow.

LORD GORING. Are you really serious?

MRS. CHEVELEY. Yes, quite serious.

LORD GORING. I should make you a very bad husband.

MRS. CHEVELEY. I don't mind bad husbands. I have had two. They amused me immensely.

LORD GORING. You mean that you amused yourself immensely, don't you?

MRS. CHEVELEY. What do you know about my married life?

LORD GORING. Nothing: but I can read it like a book.

MRS. CHEVELEY. What book?

LORD GORING. [Rising.] The Book of Numbers.

MRS. CHEVELEY. Do you think it is quite charming of you to be so rude to a woman in your own house?

LORD GORING. In the case of very fascinating women, sex is a challenge, not a defence.

MRS. CHEVELEY. I suppose that is meant for a compliment. My dear Arthur, women are never disarmed by compliments. Men always are. That is the difference between the two sexes.

LORD GORING. Women are never disarmed by anything, as far as I know them.

MRS. CHEVELEY. [After a pause.] Then you are going to allow your greatest friend, Robert Chiltern, to be ruined, rather than marry some one who really has considerable attractions left. I thought you would have risen to some great height of self-sacrifice, Arthur. I think you should. And the rest of your life you could spend in contemplating your own perfections.

LORD GORING. Oh! I do that as it is. And self-sacrifice is a thing that should be put down by law. It is so demoralising to the people for whom one sacrifices oneself. They always go to the bad.

MRS. CHEVELEY. As if anything could demoralise Robert Chiltern! You seem to forget that I know his real character.

LORD GORING. What you know about him is not his real character. It was an act of folly done in his youth, dishonourable, I admit, shameful, I admit, unworthy of him, I admit, and therefore . . . not his true character.

MRS. CHEVELEY. How you men stand up for each other!

An Ideal Husband

LORD GORING. How you women war against each other!

MRS. CHEVELEY. [Bitterly.] I only war against one woman, against Gertrude Chiltern. I hate her. I hate her now more than ever.

LORD GORING. Because you have brought a real tragedy into her life, I suppose.

MRS. CHEVELEY. [With a sneer.] Oh, there is only one real tragedy in a woman's life. The fact that her past is always her lover, and her future invariably her husband.

LORD GORING. Lady Chiltern knows nothing of the kind of life to which you are alluding.

MRS. CHEVELEY. A woman whose size in gloves is seven and three- quarters never knows much about anything. You know Gertrude has always worn seven and three-quarters? That is one of the reasons why there was never any moral sympathy between us. . . . Well, Arthur, I suppose this romantic interview may be regarded as at an end. You admit it was romantic, don't you? For the privilege of being your wife I was ready to surrender a great prize, the climax of my diplomatic career. You decline. Very well. If Sir Robert doesn't uphold my Argentine scheme, I expose him. VOILE TOUT.

LORD GORING. You mustn't do that. It would be vile, horrible, infamous.

MRS. CHEVELEY. [Shrugging her shoulders.] Oh! don't use big words. They mean so little. It is a commercial transaction. That is all. There is no good mixing up sentimentality in it. I offered to sell Robert Chiltern a certain thing. If he won't pay me my price, he will have to pay the world a greater price. There is no more to be said. I must go. Good-bye. Won't you shake hands?

LORD GORING. With you? No. Your transaction with Robert Chiltern may pass as a loathsome commercial transaction of a loathsome commercial age; but you seem to have forgotten that you came here to- night to talk of love, you whose lips desecrated the word love, you to whom the thing is a book closely sealed, went this afternoon to the house of one of the most noble and gentle women in the world to degrade her husband in her eyes, to try and kill her love for him, to put poison in her heart, and bitterness in her life, to break her idol, and, it may be, spoil her soul. That I cannot forgive you. That was horrible. For that there can be no forgiveness.

MRS. CHEVELEY. Arthur, you are unjust to me. Believe me, you are quite unjust to me. I didn't go to taunt Gertrude at all. I had no idea of doing anything of the kind when I entered. I called with Lady Markby simply to ask whether an ornament, a jewel, that I lost somewhere last night, had been found at the Chilterns'. If you don't believe me, you can ask Lady Markby. She will tell you it is true. The scene that occurred happened after Lady Markby had left, and was really forced on me by Gertrude's rudeness and sneers. I called, oh! - a little out of malice if you like - but really to ask if a diamond brooch of mine had been found. That was the origin of the whole thing.

LORD GORING. A diamond snake-brooch with a ruby?

MRS. CHEVELEY. Yes. How do you know?

LORD GORING. Because it is found. In point of fact, I found it myself, and stupidly forgot to tell the butler anything about it as I was leaving. [Goes over to the writing-table and pulls out the drawers.] It is in this drawer. No, that one. This is the brooch, isn't it? [Holds up the brooch.]

MRS. CHEVELEY. Yes. I am so glad to get it back. It was . . a present.

LORD GORING. Won't you wear it?

MRS. CHEVELEY. Certainly, if you pin it in. [LORD GORING suddenly clasps it on her arm.] Why do you put it on as a bracelet? I never knew it could he worn as a bracelet.

LORD GORING. Really?

MRS. CHEVELEY. [Holding out her handsome arm.] No; but it looks very well on me as a bracelet, doesn't it?

LORD GORING. Yes; much better than when I saw it last.

MRS. CHEVELEY. When did you see it last?

LORD GORING. [Calmly.] Oh, ten years ago, on Lady Berkshire, from whom you stole it.

MRS. CHEVELEY. [Starting.] What do you mean?

LORD GORING. I mean that you stole that ornament from my cousin, Mary Berkshire, to whom I gave it when she was married. Suspicion fell on a wretched servant, who was sent away in disgrace. I recognised it last night. I determined to say nothing about it till I had found the thief. I have found the thief now, and I have heard her own confession.

MRS. CHEVELEY. [Tossing her head.] It is not true.

LORD GORING. You know it is true. Why, thief is written across your face at this moment.

MRS. CHEVELEY. I will deny the whole affair from beginning to end. I will say that I have never seen this wretched thing, that it was never in my possession.

[MRS. CHEVELEY tries to get the bracelet off her arm, but fails. LORD GORING looks on amused. Her thin fingers tear at the jewel to no purpose. A curse breaks from her.]

LORD GORING. The drawback of stealing a thing, Mrs. Cheveley, is that one never knows how wonderful the thing that one steals is. You can't get that bracelet off, unless you know where the spring is. And I see you don't know where the spring is. It is rather difficult to find.

MRS. CHEVELEY. You brute! You coward! [She tries again to unclasp the bracelet, but fails.]

LORD GORING. Oh! don't use big words. They mean so little.

MRS. CHEVELEY. [Again tears at the bracelet in a paroxysm of rage, with inarticulate sounds. Then stops, and looks at LORD GORING.] What are you going to do?

LORD GORING. I am going to ring for my servant. He is an admirable servant. Always comes in the moment one rings for him. When he comes I will tell him to fetch the police.

MRS. CHEVELEY. [Trembling.] The police? What for?

LORD GORING. To-morrow the Berkshires will prosecute you. That is what the police are for.

MRS. CHEVELEY. [Is now in an agony of physical terror. Her face is distorted. Her mouth awry. A mask has fallen from her. She it, for the moment, dreadful to look at.] Don't do that. I will do anything you want. Anything in the world you want.

LORD GORING. Give me Robert Chiltern's letter.

MRS. CHEVELEY. Stop! Stop! Let me have time to think.

LORD GORING. Give me Robert Chiltern's letter.

MRS. CHEVELEY. I have not got it with me. I will give it to you to-morrow.

LORD GORING. You know you are lying. Give it to me at once. [MRS. CHEVELEY pulls the letter out, and hands it to him. She is horribly pale.] This is it?

MRS. CHEVELEY. [In a hoarse voice.] Yes.

LORD GORING. [Takes the letter, examines it, sighs, and burns it with the lamp.] For so well-dressed a woman, Mrs. Cheveley, you have moments of admirable common sense. I congratulate you.

MRS. CHEVELEY. [Catches sight of LADY CHILTERN'S letter, the cover of which is just showing from under the blotting-book.] Please get me a glass of water.

LORD GORING. Certainly. [Goes to the corner of the room and pours out a glass of water. While his back is turned MRS. CHEVELEY steals LADY CHILTERN'S letter. When LORD GORING returns the glass she refuses it with a gesture.]

MRS. CHEVELEY. Thank you. Will you help me on with my cloak?

LORD GORING. With pleasure. [Puts her cloak on.]

MRS. CHEVELEY. Thanks. I am never going to try to harm Robert Chiltern again.

LORD GORING. Fortunately you have not the chance, Mrs. Cheveley.

MRS. CHEVELEY. Well, if even I had the chance, I wouldn't. On the contrary, I am going to render him a great service.

LORD GORING. I am charmed to hear it. It is a reformation.

MRS. CHEVELEY. Yes. I can't bear so upright a gentleman, so honourable an English gentleman, being so shamefully deceived, and so -

LORD GORING. Well?

MRS. CHEVELEY. I find that somehow Gertrude Chiltern's dying speech and confession has strayed into my pocket.

LORD GORING. What do you mean?

MRS. CHEVELEY. [With a bitter note of triumph in her voice.] I mean that I am going to send Robert Chiltern the love-letter his wife wrote to you to-night.

LORD GORING. Love-letter?

MRS. CHEVELEY. [Laughing.] 'I want you. I trust you. I am coming to you. Gertrude.'

[LORD GORING rushes to the bureau and takes up the envelope, finds is empty, and turns round.]

LORD GORING. You wretched woman, must you always be thieving? Give me back that letter. I'll take it from you by force. You shall not leave my room till I have got it.

[He rushes towards her, but MRS. CHEVELEY at once puts her hand on the electric bell that is on the table. The bell sounds with shrill reverberations, and PHIPPS enters.]

MRS. CHEVELEY. [After a pause.] Lord Goring merely rang that you should show me out. Good-night, Lord Goring!

[Goes out followed by PHIPPS. Her face it illumined with evil triumph. There is joy in her eyes. Youth seems to have come back to her. Her last glance is like a swift arrow. LORD GORING bites his lip, and lights his a cigarette.]

ACT DROPS

FOURTH ACT

SCENE

Same as Act II.

[LORD GORING is standing by the fireplace with his hands in his pockets. He is looking rather bored.]

LORD GORING. [Pulls out his watch, inspects it, and rings the bell.] It is a great nuisance. I can't find any one in this house to talk to. And I am full of interesting information. I feel like the latest edition of something or other.

[Enter servant.]

JAMES. Sir Robert is still at the Foreign Office, my lord.

LORD GORING. Lady Chiltern not down yet?

JAMES. Her ladyship has not yet left her room. Miss Chiltern has just come in from riding.

LORD GORING. [To himself.] Ah! that is something.

JAMES. Lord Caversham has been waiting some time in the library for Sir Robert. I told him your lordship was here.

LORD GORING. Thank you! Would you kindly tell him I've gone?

JAMES. [Bowing.] I shall do so, my lord.

[Exit servant.]

LORD GORING. Really, I don't want to meet my father three days running. It is a great deal too much excitement for any son. I hope to goodness he won't come up. Fathers should be neither seen nor heard. That is the only proper basin for family life. Mothers are different. Mothers are darlings. [Throws himself down into a chair, picks up a paper and begins to read it.]

[Enter LORD CAVERSHAM.]

LORD CAVERSHAM. Well, sir, what are you doing here? Wasting your time as usual, I suppose?

LORD GORING. [Throws down paper and rises.] My dear father, when one pays a visit it is for the purpose of wasting other people's time, not one's own.

LORD CAVERSHAM. Have you been thinking over what I spoke to you about last night?

LORD GORING. I have been thinking about nothing else.

LORD CAVERSHAM. Engaged to be married yet?

LORD GORING. [Genially.] Not yet: but I hope to be before lunch-time.

LORD CAVERSHAM. [Caustically.] You can have till dinner-time if it would be of any convenience to you.

LORD GORING. Thanks awfully, but I think I'd sooner be engaged before lunch.

LORD CAVERSHAM. Humph! Never know when you are serious or not.

LORD GORING. Neither do I, father.

[A pause.]

LORD CAVERSHAM. I suppose you have read THE TIMES this morning?

LORD GORING. [Airily.] THE TIMES? Certainly not. I only read THE MORNING POST. All that one should know about modern life is where the Duchesses are; anything else is quite demoralising.

LORD CAVERSHAM. Do you mean to say you have not read THE TIMES leading article on Robert Chiltern's career?

LORD GORING. Good heavens! No. What does it say?

LORD CAVERSHAM. What should it say, sir? Everything complimentary, of course. Chiltern's speech last night on this Argentine Canal scheme was one of the finest pieces of oratory ever delivered in the House since Canning.

LORD GORING. Ah! Never heard of Canning. Never wanted to. And did . . . did Chiltern uphold the scheme?

LORD CAVERSHAM. Uphold it, sir? How little you know him! Why, he denounced it roundly, and the whole system of modern political finance. This speech is the turning-point in his career, as THE TIMES points out. You should read this article, sir. [Opens THE TIMES.] 'Sir Robert Chiltern . . . most rising of our young statesmen . . . Brilliant orator . . . Unblemished career . . . Well- known integrity of character . . . Represents what is best in English public life . . . Noble contrast to the lax morality so common among foreign politicians.' They will never say that of you, sir.

LORD GORING. I sincerely hope not, father. However, I am delighted at what you tell me about Robert, thoroughly delighted. It shows he has got pluck.

LORD CAVERSHAM. He has got more than pluck, sir, he has got genius.

LORD GORING. Ah! I prefer pluck. It is not so common, nowadays, as genius is.

LORD CAVERSHAM. I wish you would go into Parliament.

LORD GORING. My dear father, only people who look dull ever get into the House of Commons, and only people who are dull ever succeed there.

LORD CAVERSHAM. Why don't you try to do something useful in life?

LORD GORING. I am far too young.

LORD CAVERSHAM. [Testily.] I hate this affectation of youth, sir. It is a great deal too prevalent nowadays.

LORD GORING. Youth isn't an affectation. Youth is an art.

LORD CAVERSHAM. Why don't you propose to that pretty Miss Chiltern?

LORD GORING. I am of a very nervous disposition, especially in the morning.

LORD CAVERSHAM. I don't suppose there is the smallest chance of her accepting you.

LORD GORING. I don't know how the betting stands to-day.

LORD CAVERSHAM. If she did accept you she would be the prettiest fool in England.

LORD GORING. That is just what I should like to marry. A thoroughly sensible wife would reduce me to a condition of absolute idiocy in less than six months.

LORD CAVERSHAM. You don't deserve her, sir.

LORD GORING. My dear father, if we men married the women we deserved, we should have a very bad time of it.

[Enter MABEL CHILTERN.]

MABEL CHILTERN. Oh! . . . How do you do, Lord Caversham? I hope Lady Caversham is quite well?

LORD CAVERSHAM. Lady Caversham is as usual, as usual.

LORD GORING. Good morning, Miss Mabel!

MABEL CHILTERN. [Taking no notice at all of LORD GORING, and addressing herself exclusively to LORD CAVERSHAM.] And Lady Caversham's bonnets . . . are they at all better?

LORD CAVERSHAM. They have had a serious relapse, I am sorry to say.

LORD GORING. Good morning, Miss Mabel!

MABEL CHILTERN. [To LORD CAVERSHAM.] I hope an operation will not be necessary.

LORD CAVERSHAM. [Smiling at her pertness.] If it is, we shall have to give Lady Caversham a narcotic. Otherwise she would never consent to have a feather touched.

LORD GORING. [With increased emphasis.] Good morning, Miss Mabel!

MABEL CHILTERN. [Turning round with feigned surprise.] Oh, are you here? Of course you understand that after your breaking your appointment I am never going to speak to you again.

LORD GORING. Oh, please don't say such a thing. You are the one person in London I really like to have to listen to me.

MABEL CHILTERN. Lord Goring, I never believe a single word that either you or I say to each other.

LORD CAVERSHAM. You are quite right, my dear, quite right . . . as far as he is concerned, I mean.

MABEL CHILTERN. Do you think you could possibly make your son behave a little better occasionally? Just as a change.

LORD CAVERSHAM. I regret to say, Miss Chiltern, that I have no influence at all over my son. I wish I had. If I had, I know what I would make him do.

MABEL CHILTERN. I am afraid that he has one of those terribly weak natures that are not susceptible to influence.

LORD CAVERSHAM. He is very heartless, very heartless.

LORD GORING. It seems to me that I am a little in the way here.

MABEL CHILTERN. It is very good for you to be in the way, and to know what people say of you behind your back.

LORD GORING. I don't at all like knowing what people say of me behind my back. It makes me far too conceited.

LORD CAVERSHAM. After that, my dear, I really must bid you good morning.

MABEL CHILTERN. Oh! I hope you are not going to leave me all alone with Lord Goring? Especially at such an early hour in the day.

LORD CAVERSHAM. I am afraid I can't take him with me to Downing Street. It is not the Prime Minster's day for seeing the unemployed.

[Shakes hands with MABEL CHILTERN, takes up his hat and stick, and goes out, with a parting glare of indignation at LORD GORING.]

MABEL CHILTERN. [Takes up roses and begins to arrange them in a bowl on the table.] People who don't keep their appointments in the Park are horrid.

LORD GORING. Detestable.

MABEL CHILTERN. I am glad you admit it. But I wish you wouldn't look so pleased about it.

LORD GORING. I can't help it. I always look pleased when I am with you.

MABEL CHILTERN. [Sadly.] Then I suppose it is my duty to remain with you?

LORD GORING. Of course it is.

MABEL CHILTERN. Well, my duty is a thing I never do, on principle. It always depresses me. So I am afraid I must leave you.

LORD GORING. Please don't, Miss Mabel. I have something very particular to say to you.

MABEL CHILTERN. [Rapturously.] Oh! is it a proposal?

LORD GORING. [Somewhat taken aback.] Well, yes, it is - I am bound to say it is.

MABEL CHILTERN. [With a sigh of pleasure.] I am so glad. That makes the second to-day.

LORD GORING. [Indignantly.] The second to-day? What conceited ass has been impertinent enough to dare to propose to you before I had proposed to you?

MABEL CHILTERN. Tommy Trafford, of course. It is one of Tommy's days for proposing. He always proposes on Tuesdays and Thursdays, during the Season.

LORD GORING. You didn't accept him, I hope?

MABEL CHILTERN. I make it a rule never to accept Tommy. That is why he goes on proposing. Of course, as you didn't turn up this morning, I very nearly said yes. It would have been an excellent lesson both for him and for you if I had. It would have taught you both better manners.

LORD GORING. Oh! bother Tommy Trafford. Tommy is a silly little ass. I love you.

MABEL CHILTERN. I know. And I think you might have mentioned it before. I am sure I have given you heaps of opportunities.

LORD GORING. Mabel, do be serious. Please be serious.

MABEL CHILTERN. Ah! that is the sort of thing a man always says to a girl before he has been married to her. He never says it afterwards.

LORD GORING. [Taking hold of her hand.] Mabel, I have told you that I love you. Can't you love me a little in return?

MABEL CHILTERN. You silly Arthur! If you knew anything about . . . anything, which you don't, you would know that I adore you. Every one in London knows it except you. It is a public scandal the way I adore you. I have been going about for the last six months telling the whole of society that I adore you. I wonder you consent to have anything to say to me. I have no character left at all. At least, I feel so happy that I am quite sure I have no character left at all.

LORD GORING. [Catches her in his arms and kisses her. Then there is a pause of bliss.] Dear! Do you know I was awfully afraid of being refused!

MABEL CHILTERN. [Looking up at him.] But you never have been refused yet by anybody, have you, Arthur? I can't imagine any one refusing you.

LORD GORING. [After kissing her again.] Of course I'm not nearly good enough for you, Mabel.

MABEL CHILTERN. [Nestling close to him.] I am so glad, darling. I was afraid you were.

LORD GORING. [After some hesitation.] And I'm . . . I'm a little over thirty.

MABEL CHILTERN. Dear, you look weeks younger than that.

LORD GORING. [Enthusiastically.] How sweet of you to say so! . . . And it is only fair to tell you frankly that I am fearfully extravagant.

MABEL CHILTERN. But so am I, Arthur. So we're sure to agree. And now I must go and see Gertrude.

LORD GORING. Must you really? [Kisses her.]

MABEL CHILTERN. Yes.

LORD GORING. Then do tell her I want to talk to her particularly. I have been waiting here all the morning to see either her or Robert.

MABEL CHILTERN. Do you mean to say you didn't come here expressly to propose to me?

LORD GORING. [Triumphantly.] No; that was a flash of genius.

MABEL CHILTERN. Your first.

LORD GORING. [With determination.] My last.

MABEL CHILTERN. I am delighted to hear it. Now don't stir. I'll be back in five minutes. And don't fall into any temptations while I am away.

LORD GORING. Dear Mabel, while you are away, there are none. It makes me horribly dependent on you.

[Enter LADY CHILTERN.]

LADY CHILTERN. Good morning, dear! How pretty you are looking!

MABEL CHILTERN. How pale you are looking, Gertrude! It is most becoming!

LADY CHILTERN. Good morning, Lord Goring!

LORD GORING. [Bowing.] Good morning, Lady Chiltern!

MABEL CHILTERN. [Aside to LORD GORING.] I shall be in the conservatory under the second palm tree on the left.

LORD GORING. Second on the left?

MABEL CHILTERN. [With a look of mock surprise.] Yes; the usual palm tree.

[Blows a kiss to him, unobserved by LADY CHILTERN, and goes out.]

LORD GORING. Lady Chiltern, I have a certain amount of very good news to tell you. Mrs. Cheveley gave me up Robert's letter last night, and I burned it. Robert is safe.

LADY CHILTERN. [Sinking on the sofa.] Safe! Oh! I am so glad of that. What a good friend you are to him - to us!

LORD GORING. There is only one person now that could be said to be in any danger.

LADY CHILTERN. Who is that?

LORD GORING. [Sitting down beside her.] Yourself.

LADY CHILTERN. I? In danger? What do you mean?

LORD GORING. Danger is too great a word. It is a word I should not have used. But I admit I have something to tell you that may distress you, that terribly distresses me. Yesterday evening you wrote me a very beautiful, womanly letter, asking me for my help. You wrote to me as one of your oldest friends, one of your husband's oldest friends. Mrs. Cheveley stole that letter from my rooms.

LADY CHILTERN. Well, what use is it to her? Why should she not have it?

LORD GORING. [Rising.] Lady Chiltern, I will be quite frank with you. Mrs. Cheveley puts a certain construction on that letter and proposes to send it to your husband.

LADY CHILTERN. But what construction could she put on it? . . . Oh! not that! not that! If I in - in trouble, and wanting your help, trusting you, propose to come to you . . . that you may advise me . . . assist me . . . Oh! are there women so horrible as that . . .? And she proposes to send it to my husband? Tell me what happened. Tell me all that happened.

LORD GORING. Mrs. Cheveley was concealed in a room adjoining my library, without my knowledge. I thought that the person who was waiting in that room to see me was yourself. Robert came in unexpectedly. A chair or something fell in the room. He forced his way in, and he discovered her. We had a terrible scene. I still thought it was you. He left me in anger. At the end of everything Mrs. Cheveley got possession of your letter - she stole it, when or how, I don't know.

LADY CHILTERN. At what hour did this happen?

LORD GORING. At half-past ten. And now I propose that we tell Robert the whole thing at once.

LADY CHILTERN. [Looking at him with amazement that is almost terror.] You want me to tell Robert that the woman you expected was not Mrs. Cheveley, but myself? That it was I whom you thought was concealed in a room in your house, at half-past ten o'clock at night? You want me to tell him that?

LORD GORING. I think it is better that he should know the exact truth.

LADY CHILTERN. [Rising.] Oh, I couldn't, I couldn't!

LORD GORING. May I do it?

LADY CHILTERN. No.

LORD GORING. [Gravely.] You are wrong, Lady Chiltern.

LADY CHILTERN. No. The letter must be intercepted. That is all. But how can I do it? Letters arrive for him every moment of the day. His secretaries open them and hand them to him. I dare not ask the servants to bring me his letters. It would be impossible. Oh! why don't you tell me what to do?

LORD GORING. Pray be calm, Lady Chiltern, and answer the questions I am going to put to you. You said his secretaries open his letters.

LADY CHILTERN. Yes.

LORD GORING. Who is with him to-day? Mr. Trafford, isn't it?

LADY CHILTERN. No. Mr. Montford, I think.

LORD GORING. You can trust him?

LADY CHILTERN. [With a gesture of despair.] Oh! how do I know?

LORD GORING. He would do what you asked him, wouldn't he?

LADY CHILTERN. I think so.

LORD GORING. Your letter was on pink paper. He could recognise it without reading it, couldn't he? By the colour?

LADY CHILTERN. I suppose so.

LORD GORING. Is he in the house now?

LADY CHILTERN. Yes.

LORD GORING. Then I will go and see him myself, and tell him that a certain letter, written on pink paper, is to be forwarded to Robert to-day, and that at all costs it must not reach him. [Goes to the door, and opens it.] Oh! Robert is coming upstairs with the letter in his hand. It has reached him already.

LADY CHILTERN. [With a cry of pain.] Oh! you have saved his life; what have you done with mine?

[Enter SIR ROBERT CHILTERN. He has the letter in his hand, and is reading it. He comes towards his wife, not noticing LORD GORING'S presence.]

SIR ROBERT CHILTERN. 'I want you. I trust you. I am coming to you. Gertrude.' Oh, my love! Is this true? Do you indeed trust me, and want me? If so, it was for me to come to you, not for you to write of coming to me. This letter of yours, Gertrude, makes me feel that nothing that the world may do can hurt me now. You want me, Gertrude?

[LORD GORING, unseen by SIR ROBERT CHILTERN, makes an imploring sign to LADY CHILTERN to accept the situation and SIR ROBERT'S error.]

LADY CHILTERN. Yes.

SIR ROBERT CHILTERN. You trust me, Gertrude?

LADY CHILTERN. Yes.

SIR ROBERT CHILTERN. Ah! why did you not add you loved me?

LADY CHILTERN. [Taking his hand.] Because I loved you.

[LORD GORING passes into the conservatory.]

SIR ROBERT CHILTERN. [Kisses her.] Gertrude, you don't know what I feel. When Montford passed me your letter across the table - he had opened it by mistake, I suppose, without looking at the handwriting on the envelope - and I read it - oh! I did not care what disgrace or punishment was in store for me, I only thought you loved me still.

LADY CHILTERN. There is no disgrace in store for you, nor any public shame. Mrs. Cheveley has handed over to Lord Goring the document that was in her possession, and he has destroyed it.

SIR ROBERT CHILTERN. Are you sure of this, Gertrude?

LADY CHILTERN. Yes; Lord Goring has just told me.

SIR ROBERT CHILTERN. Then I am safe! Oh! what a wonderful thing to be safe! For two days I have been in terror. I am safe now. How did Arthur destroy my letter? Tell me.

LADY CHILTERN. He burned it.

SIR ROBERT CHILTERN. I wish I had seen that one sin of my youth burning to ashes. How many men there are in modern life who would like to see their past burning to white ashes before them! Is Arthur still here?

LADY CHILTERN. Yes; he is in the conservatory.

SIR ROBERT CHILTERN. I am so glad now I made that speech last night in the House, so glad. I made it thinking that public disgrace might be the result. But it has not been so.

LADY CHILTERN. Public honour has been the result.

SIR ROBERT CHILTERN. I think so. I fear so, almost. For although I am safe from detection, although every proof against me is destroyed, I suppose, Gertrude . . . I suppose I should retire from public life? [He looks anxiously at his wife.]

LADY CHILTERN. [Eagerly.] Oh yes, Robert, you should do that. It is your duty to do that.

SIR ROBERT CHILTERN. It is much to surrender.

LADY CHILTERN. No; it will be much to gain.

[SIR ROBERT CHILTERN walks up and down the room with a troubled expression. Then comes over to his wife, and puts his hand on her shoulder.]

SIR ROBERT CHILTERN. And you would be happy living somewhere alone with me, abroad perhaps, or in the country away from London, away from public life? You would have no regrets?

LADY CHILTERN. Oh! none, Robert.

SIR ROBERT CHILTERN. [Sadly.] And your ambition for me? You used to be ambitious for me.

LADY CHILTERN. Oh, my ambition! I have none now, but that we two may love each other. It was your ambition that led you astray. Let us not talk about ambition.

[LORD GORING returns from the conservatory, looking very pleased with himself, and with an entirely new buttonhole that some one has made for him.]

SIR ROBERT CHILTERN. [Going towards him.] Arthur, I have to thank you for what you have done for me. I don't know how I can repay you. [Shakes hands with him.]

LORD GORING. My dear fellow, I'll tell you at once. At the present moment, under the usual palm tree . . . I mean in the conservatory . . .

[Enter MASON.]

MASON. Lord Caversham.

LORD GORING. That admirable father of mine really makes a habit of turning up at the wrong moment. It is very heartless of him, very heartless indeed.

[Enter LORD CAVERSHAM. MASON goes out.]

LORD CAVERSHAM. Good morning, Lady Chiltern! Warmest congratulations to you, Chiltern, on your brilliant speech last night. I have just left the Prime Minister, and you are to have the vacant seat in the Cabinet.

SIR ROBERT CHILTERN. [With a look of joy and triumph.] A seat in the Cabinet?

LORD CAVERSHAM. Yes; here is the Prime Minister's letter. [Hands letter.]

SIR ROBERT CHILTERN. [Takes letter and reads it.] A seat in the Cabinet!

LORD CAVERSHAM. Certainly, and you well deserve it too. You have got what we want so much in political life nowadays - high character, high moral tone, high principles. [To LORD GORING.] Everything that you have not got, sir, and never will have.

LORD GORING. I don't like principles, father. I prefer prejudices.

[SIR ROBERT CHILTERN is on the brink of accepting the Prime Minister's offer, when he sees wife looking at him with her clear, candid eyes. He then realises that it is impossible.]

SIR ROBERT CHILTERN. I cannot accept this offer, Lord Caversham. I have made up my mind to decline it.

LORD CAVERSHAM. Decline it, sir!

SIR ROBERT CHILTERN. My intention is to retire at once from public life.

LORD CAVERSHAM. [Angrily.] Decline a seat in the Cabinet, and retire from public life? Never heard such damned nonsense in the whole course of my existence. I beg your pardon, Lady Chiltern. Chiltern, I beg your pardon. [To LORD GORING.] Don't grin like that, sir.

LORD GORING. No, father.

LORD CAVERSHAM. Lady Chiltern, you are a sensible woman, the most sensible woman in London, the most sensible woman I know. Will you kindly prevent your husband from making such a . . . from taking such . . . Will you kindly do that, Lady Chiltern?

LADY CHILTERN. I think my husband in right in his determination, Lord Caversham. I approve of it.

LORD CAVERSHAM. You approve of it? Good heavens!

LADY CHILTERN. [Taking her husband's hand.] I admire him for it. I admire him immensely for it. I have never admired him so much before. He is finer than even I thought him. [To SIR ROBERT CHILTERN.] You will go and write your letter to the Prime Minister now, won't you? Don't hesitate about it, Robert.

SIR ROBERT CHILTERN. [With a touch of bitterness.] I suppose I had better write it at once. Such offers are not repeated. I will ask you to excuse me for a moment, Lord Caversham.

LADY CHILTERN. I may come with you, Robert, may I not?

SIR ROBERT CHILTERN. Yes, Gertrude.

[LADY CHILTERN goes out with him.]

LORD CAVERSHAM. What is the matter with this family? Something wrong here, eh? [Tapping his forehead.] Idiocy? Hereditary, I suppose. Both of them, too. Wife as well as husband. Very sad. Very sad indeed! And they are not an old family. Can't understand it.

LORD GORING. It is not idiocy, father, I assure you.

LORD CAVERSHAM. What is it then, sir?

LORD GORING. [After some hesitation.] Well, it is what is called nowadays a high moral tone, father. That is all.

LORD CAVERSHAM. Hate these new-fangled names. Same thing as we used to call idiocy fifty years ago. Shan't stay in this house any longer.

LORD GORING. [Taking his arm.] Oh! just go in here for a moment, father. Third palm tree to the left, the usual palm tree.

LORD CAVERSHAM. What, sir?

LORD GORING. I beg your pardon, father, I forgot. The conservatory, father, the conservatory - there is some one there I want you to talk to.

LORD CAVERSHAM. What about, sir?

LORD GORING. About me, father,

LORD CAVERSHAM. [Grimly.] Not a subject on which much eloquence is possible.

LORD GORING. No, father; but the lady is like me. She doesn't care much for eloquence in others. She thinks it a little loud.

[LORD CAVERSHAM goes out into the conservatory. LADY CHILTERN enters.]

LORD GORING. Lady Chiltern, why are you playing Mrs. Cheveley's cards?

LADY CHILTERN. [Startled.] I don't understand you.

LORD GORING. Mrs. Cheveley made an attempt to ruin your husband. Either to drive him from public life, or to make him adopt a dishonourable position. From the latter tragedy you saved him. The former you are now thrusting on him. Why should you do him the wrong Mrs. Cheveley tried to do and failed?

LADY CHILTERN. Lord Goring?

LORD GORING. [Pulling himself together for a great effort, and showing the philosopher that underlies the dandy.] Lady Chiltern, allow me. You wrote me a letter last night in which you said you trusted me and wanted my help. Now is the moment when you really want my help, now is the time when you have got to trust me, to trust in my counsel and judgment. You love Robert. Do you want to kill his love for you? What sort of existence will he have if you rob him of the fruits of his ambition, if you take him from the splendour of a great political career, if you close the doors of public life against him, if you condemn him to sterile failure, he who was made for triumph and success? Women are not meant to judge us, but to forgive us when we need forgiveness. Pardon, not punishment, is their mission. Why should you scourge him with rods for a sin done in his youth, before he knew you, before he knew himself? A man's life is of more value than a woman's. It has larger issues, wider scope, greater ambitions. A woman's life revolves in curves of emotions. It is upon lines of intellect that a man's life progresses. Don't make any terrible mistake, Lady Chiltern. A woman who can

An Ideal Husband

keep a man's love, and love him in return, has done all the world
wants of women, or should want of them.

LADY CHILTERN. [Troubled and hesitating.] But it is my husband
himself who wishes to retire from public life. He feels it is his duty. It
was he who first said so.

LORD GORING. Rather than lose your love, Robert would do
anything, wreck his whole career, as he is on the brink of doing now.
He is making for you a terrible sacrifice. Take my advice, Lady
Chiltern, and do not accept a sacrifice so great. If you do, you will
live to repent it bitterly. We men and women are not made to accept
such sacrifices from each other. We are not worthy of them. Besides,
Robert has been punished enough.

LADY CHILTERN. We have both been punished. I set him up too
high.

LORD GORING. [With deep feeling in his voice.] Do not for that
reason set him down now too low. If he has fallen from his altar, do
not thrust him into the mire. Failure to Robert would be the very
mire of shame. Power is his passion. He would lose everything, even
his power to feel love. Your husband's life is at this moment in your
hands, your husband's love is in your hands. Don't mar both for
him.

[Enter SIR ROBERT CHILTERN.]

SIR ROBERT CHILTERN. Gertrude, here is the draft of my letter.
Shall I read it to you?

LADY CHILTERN. Let me see it.

[SIR ROBERT hands her the letter. She reads it, and then, with a
gesture of passion, tears it up.]

SIR ROBERT CHILTERN. What are you doing?

LADY CHILTERN. A man's life is of more value than a woman's. It
has larger issues, wider scope, greater ambitions. Our lives revolve
in curves of emotions. It is upon lines of intellect that a man's life
progresses. I have just learnt this, and much else with it, from Lord

An Ideal Husband

Goring. And I will not spoil your life for you, nor see you spoil it as a sacrifice to me, a useless sacrifice!

SIR ROBERT CHILTERN. Gertrude! Gertrude!

LADY CHILTERN. You can forget. Men easily forget. And I forgive. That is how women help the world. I see that now.

SIR ROBERT CHILTERN. [Deeply overcome by emotion, embraces her.] My wife! my wife! [To LORD GORING.] Arthur, it seems that I am always to be in your debt.

LORD GORING. Oh dear no, Robert. Your debt is to Lady Chiltern, not to me!

SIR ROBERT CHILTERN. I owe you much. And now tell me what you were going to ask me just now as Lord Caversham came in.

LORD GORING. Robert, you are your sister's guardian, and I want your consent to my marriage with her. That is all.

LADY CHILTERN. Oh, I am so glad! I am so glad! [Shakes hands with LORD GORING.]

LORD GORING. Thank you, Lady Chiltern.

SIR ROBERT CHILTERN. [With a troubled look.] My sister to be your wife?

LORD GORING. Yes.

SIR ROBERT CHILTERN. [Speaking with great firmness.] Arthur, I am very sorry, but the thing is quite out of the question. I have to think of Mabel's future happiness. And I don't think her happiness would be safe in your hands. And I cannot have her sacrificed!

LORD GORING. Sacrificed!

SIR ROBERT CHILTERN. Yes, utterly sacrificed. Loveless marriages are horrible. But there is one thing worse than an absolutely loveless marriage. A marriage in which there is love, but on one side only; faith, but on one side only; devotion, but on one side only, and in which of the two hearts one is sure to be broken.

LORD GORING. But I love Mabel. No other woman has any place in my life.

LADY CHILTERN. Robert, if they love each other, why should they not be married?

SIR ROBERT CHILTERN. Arthur cannot bring Mabel the love that she deserves.

LORD GORING. What reason have you for saying that?

SIR ROBERT CHILTERN. [After a pause.] Do you really require me to tell you?

LORD GORING. Certainly I do.

SIR ROBERT CHILTERN. As you choose. When I called on you yesterday evening I found Mrs. Cheveley concealed in your rooms. It was between ten and eleven o'clock at night. I do not wish to say anything more. Your relations with Mrs. Cheveley have, as I said to you last night, nothing whatsoever to do with me. I know you were engaged to be married to her once. The fascination she exercised over you then seems to have returned. You spoke to me last night of her as of a woman pure and stainless, a woman whom you respected and honoured. That may be so. But I cannot give my sister's life into your hands. It would be wrong of me. It would be unjust, infamously unjust to her.

LORD GORING. I have nothing more to say.

LADY CHILTERN. Robert, it was not Mrs. Cheveley whom Lord Goring expected last night.

SIR ROBERT CHILTERN. Not Mrs. Cheveley! Who was it then?

LORD GORING. Lady Chiltern!

LADY CHILTERN. It was your own wife. Robert, yesterday afternoon Lord Goring told me that if ever I was in trouble I could come to him for help, as he was our oldest and best friend. Later on, after that terrible scene in this room, I wrote to him telling him that I trusted him, that I had need of him, that I was coming to him for help and advice. [SIR ROBERT CHILTERN takes the letter out of his pocket.] Yes, that letter. I didn't go to Lord Goring's, after all. I felt that it is from ourselves alone that help can come. Pride made me think that. Mrs. Cheveley went. She stole my letter and sent it anonymously to you this morning, that you should think . . . Oh! Robert, I cannot tell you what she wished you to think. . . .

SIR ROBERT CHILTERN. What! Had I fallen so low in your eyes that you thought that even for a moment I could have doubted your goodness? Gertrude, Gertrude, you are to me the white image of all good things, and sin can never touch you. Arthur, you can go to Mabel, and you have my best wishes! Oh! stop a moment. There is no name at the beginning of this letter. The brilliant Mrs. Cheveley does not seem to have noticed that. There should be a name.

LADY CHILTERN. Let me write yours. It is you I trust and need. You and none else.

LORD GORING. Well, really, Lady Chiltern, I think I should have back my own letter.

LADY CHILTERN. [Smiling.] No; you shall have Mabel. [Takes the letter and writes her husband's name on it.]

LORD GORING. Well, I hope she hasn't changed her mind. It's nearly twenty minutes since I saw her last.

[Enter MABEL CHILTERN and LORD CAVERSHAM.]

MABEL CHILTERN. Lord Goring, I think your father's conversation much more improving than yours. I am only going to talk to Lord Caversham in the future, and always under the usual palm tree.

LORD GORING. Darling! [Kisses her.]

LORD CAVERSHAM. [Considerably taken aback.] What does this mean, sir? You don't mean to say that this charming, clever young lady has been so foolish as to accept you?

LORD GORING. Certainly, father! And Chiltern's been wise enough to accept the seat in the Cabinet.

An Ideal Husband

LORD CAVERSHAM. I am very glad to hear that, Chiltern . . . I congratulate you, sir. If the country doesn't go to the dogs or the Radicals, we shall have you Prime Minister, some day.

[Enter MASON.]

MASON. Luncheon is on the table, my Lady!

[MASON goes out.]

MABEL CHILTERN. You'll stop to luncheon, Lord Caversham, won't you?

LORD CAVERSHAM. With pleasure, and I'll drive you down to Downing Street afterwards, Chiltern. You have a great future before you, a great future. Wish I could say the same for you, sir. [To LORD GORING.] But your career will have to be entirely domestic.

LORD GORING. Yes, father, I prefer it domestic.

LORD CAVERSHAM. And if you don't make this young lady an ideal husband, I'll cut you off with a shilling.

MABEL CHILTERN. An ideal husband! Oh, I don't think I should like that. It sounds like something in the next world.

LORD CAVERSHAM. What do you want him to be then, dear?

MABEL CHILTERN. He can be what he chooses. All I want is to be . . . to be . . . oh! a real wife to him.

LORD CAVERSHAM. Upon my word, there is a good deal of common sense in that, Lady Chiltern.

[They all go out except SIR ROBERT CHILTERN. He sinks in a chair, wrapt in thought. After a little time LADY CHILTERN returns to look for him.]

LADY CHILTERN. [Leaning over the back of the chair.] Aren't you coming in, Robert?

SIR ROBERT CHILTERN. [Taking her hand.] Gertrude, is it love you feel for me, or is it pity merely?

LADY CHILTERN. [Kisses him.] It is love, Robert. Love, and only love. For both of us a new life is beginning.

CURTAIN